Anyone

14-

NU

AU

......

TIT

....

...

D1419946

This book may be recalled before the above date.

Anyone for *Alpha?*

Evangelism in a
Post-Christian Society

Stephen Hunt

DARTON·LONGMAN + TODD

First published in 2001 by
Darton, Longman and Todd Ltd
1 Spencer Court
140-142 Wandsworth High Street
London SW18 4JJ

ISBN 0–232–52404–1

A catalogue record for this book is available from the British Library.

Designed by Sandie Boccacci
Phototypeset 9/12¼pt Bookman Light by Intype London Ltd
Printed and bound in Great Britain by
Page Bros, Norwich

1 00367 4057

Contents

Contents

Foreword

The 1990s in Britain was, among many other things, the 'decade of evangelism'. The call to worldwide 'evangelisation' had been made by Pope John Paul as a call to Christian effort and commitment leading to the millennial (or Jubilee) celebration of the birth of Christ. Tacitly supported by the Archbishop of Canterbury and enthusiastically backed by Protestant evangelicals, the 'decade of evangelism' was a battle cry of engagement with the secular forces of modernity.

The problem was that mainline churches in the 1960s and early 1970s had either embraced secularity with enthusiasm (especially those enamoured with Harvey Cox's thesis of the 'Secular City') or they had become timid before the seemingly inexorable secularisation of religion in the twentieth century. Bishop Lesslie Newbigin, having retired to England from thirty years' missionary service in India, wrote a booklet for the British Council of Churches in 1983 entitled *The Other Side of 84* in which he virtually accused the churches of reneging on the gospel.

But it was not only the more liberal churches that were at odds with an evangelistic agenda. I recall being asked by Dr Philip Morgan, the General Secretary of the British Council of Churches in the 1980s, to make up a panel to appoint someone to run the new evangelistic committee. Our chosen candidate was from the Salvation Army. He was honest enough to admit that the SA itself did not really know how to evangelise any more: arguably its roots in the holiness traditions of the nineteenth century had been weakened, so that welfare work, the vending of *War Cry* and marching brass bands to public and private functions had overwhelmed the call to salvation.

The evangelical wing of the Church of England, Baptist assemblies, and Pentecostal churches remained committed to evangelism in principle throughout the 1980s (though Methodists less so) but, like the SA, found it hard to mount successful evangelistic forays into the secular world. In the early 1960s a relatively successful approach among university students had been the mixture of prayer, Bible readings, and apologetical defence of Christianity in the Christian Union organisation. While the more liberal (but now defunct) Student Christian Movement had swallowed a cocktail of Cox, Christ and Socialism, the Christian Union were feasting on Bible notes, the writings of C. S. Lewis, John Stott, vicar of All Saints, Langham Place, London, and Francis Schaeffer, the Swiss reformed fundamentalist founder of the L'Abri organisation. The Christian Union may have made few inroads into political and social life, but it did recuit evangelical leaders who were to find their way into pastorates and positions of leadership in the 1970s and 1980s. The Revd Nicky Gumbel, curate of Holy Trinity, Brompton and the 'front man' of Alpha, took this route.

Leaders are one thing, however, but what about the rank and file, both middle and working class? And it is here that we note a curious feature of evangelical practice, namely that until the last few years, evangelists have either followed the slow, laborious and relatively fruitless task of door-to-door salesmen (now almost entirely the province of Mormons and Jehovah's Witnesses) or they have followed the nineteenth-century tradition of urban missions pioneered in America by D L Moody.[1] The urban mission was a formatted campaign or 'crusade' where the evangelist would advertise the preaching of the gospel at a special venue. Preaching was vernacular, singing demotic, and the sermon would end with an altar call at which people would come forward to be converted, counselled and forwarded to a local evangelical church if they were not already members.

After the outbreak of Pentecostal revival at Azuza Street in California in 1906, some evangelistic crusades added 'signs and wonders', such as healings and prophecies, to the preaching of the gospel. In Great Britain in the 1920s and the 1930s, the indigenous Pentecostal churches of Elim and the Assemblies of God had some success among the working class with what they liked to call the 'full gospel'. The evangelistic crusade, however, whether with Pentecostal signs or without them, became almost *de rigueur* in evangelistic circles well into the last half of the twentieth century.

Perhaps the most successful evangelistic campaign in Britain was Billy Graham's Haringey Crusade of 1953. At least it was successful in terms of ecumenical backing, media coverage, and people in large numbers getting out of their seats and going forward to the front 'to be saved'. Billy Graham was to have several pretenders to his throne in later years. Eric Hutchins, a member of the Brethren church, was to have minor success in the 1960s, and Luis Palau, an Argentinian evangelist, a greater impact in the 1980s. Since his heyday of the 1950s Billy Graham himself has visited Britain from time to time with his usual entourage. Even as late as 1984 in Mission England he was able to fill stadiums and convention centres.

But all this worthy endeavour has to be seen in the context that however enthusiastic evangelistic enterprises have been in Great Britain, relatively few people have heeded the gospel call. Evangelistic churches remain vibrant and committed but society itself has become seemingly irreversibly secular. Christianity, as measured by church attendance, has been in decline since the nineteenth century and the general consensus of polls and surveys since the 1989 English Church Census suggests that only between 9% to 12% of the population regularly attends church.[2] If we look at the best-known statistical survey of church attendance in the 1990s, Peter

Brierley's *UK Christian Handbook*, we can find evidence of relative church growth, as measured by recycled Christians from one church to another, but not of absolute growth. A pessimistic Archbishop of Canterbury, speaking only months after the end of the decade of evangelism, gloomily pronounced Britain 'a society of atheists'.

From the 1960s to the 1990s a fascination with religious experience and happy sing-along songs, has dominated the evangelical world, so that out of the million or so evangelicals that the Evangelical Alliance has claimed to represent since the late 1980s, well over half to 65% could be characterised as charismatic or neo-Pentecostal. A more dramatic and supernatural Christianity has resulted: the spectacular ministry of Californian John Wimber from the mid-1980s and the 'Toronto Blessing' of the mid-1990s comes to mind.

Ironically, at the beginning of the decade of evangelism it was, as Dr Hunt tells us, two classical Pentecostals who (a) broke with the obsession with experience that had dominated evangelical life in the 1980s, and (b) turned their back upon the much-loved evangelical formula of the crusade. Bravely, Wyn Lewis of Elim spearheaded a missionary advertising campaign, allegedly costing several millions, called JIM (Jesus In Me). But the posters and pictures were too enigmatic, and the language too archaic, to grab the attention of busy commuters and magazine browsers, and the initiative was unsuccessful. A South African evangelist, Reinhard Bonnke, was responsible for the booklet *Minus to Plus*, which was posted through the letterbox of millions of British householders. In so far that he succeeded in this postal aim, Bonnke can be said to have hit the mark, but his scattershot approach was a dubious method of 'hitting' the main evangelical target – to win converts.

Arguably, the successes of revivalism in turning back the secular tide have always been exaggerated by its proponents, but even if this is unfair, the increasingly heterogeneous nature of British culture has meant that a standard religiosity can no longer be taken for granted: religion, like the leisure industry, has to cater for a myriad of lifestyles and competing tastes. The secular world has increasingly gone over to niche marketing in its advertising methods because there is a recognition that there is no longer a homogenous popular culture as there was even in the 1960s. And this brings us to *Alpha*, the focus of this book by Stephen Hunt.

Alpha has been the surprise success story of mission at the end of the evangelistic decade and this, like the Pentecostal experiments at the beginning of the 1990s, is not without its irony. Holy Trinity, Brompton, the birthplace of *Alpha*, is a well-heeled evangelical church in the heart of London that has been the charismatic centre of the Church of England in the 1980s. Think of Wimber and 'Toronto' and you think of HTB. And yet it is from this church, reowned for its theandrical therapy rather than for its theology, that a highly structured evangelistic process has been successfully launched which has confounded its critics. *Alpha*, with its familiar and franchised logo, has taken Britain and, increasingly, America by storm. I was lecturing in First United Methodist Church, Tulsa, in April 2000, and everyone wanted to know if I knew Nicky Gumbel personally because they had all been doing *Alpha* and had taken to Gumbel's Etonian bearing and English mannerisms as if he were a local 'good ol' boy'.

Alpha advertises its wares in the 'just looking' tradition. The invition to 'come see', like the posters of the School of Economic Science lectures on the London Underground some years ago, stimulates your curiosity and offers the possibility for both knowledge and personal growth. *Alpha* itself is part evangelistic proclamation, part catechesis (Roman Catholics will hear echoes of the Rite of Christian Initiation of Adults – RCIA). Unlike the proclamation model of urban mission, with its crisis call to repent on the spot or be damned for all eternity, *Alpha* is more of a process approach to evangelism. It has little in common with 'anxious benches', sermons on perdition, and altar calls, and is more in line with Professor Abraham's model of Christian initiation – conversion (experiential), baptism (communal), love (moral), creed (cognitive), gifts of the Spirit (operational), disciplines (Eucharist), etc.[3] Perhaps, it might be argued, *Alpha* is stronger on conversion, love and gifts than cognitive, communal and disciplinary processes, but no doubt this can be compensated for as we move towards *beta, gamma* and *delta* in the immediate future (or, more likely, *Alpha* 2, 3, and 4).

But what is *Alpha,* what is the background to it, does it work, and if so *how* does it work? Is it legimate persuasion or brainwashing? Is it missiology in the market place, or a mish-mash theology for a postmodern world? In the light of these questions I recommend this study by Stephen Hunt. It is admirably rigorous in its methodology but modest in its claims – more research will be needed over several years to get a full picture (are, for example, new converts really new, and do they stay over time?). Dr Hunt makes no pretence of a theological assessment in this study but the potentially reductionist structure of his sociological approach is offset by the warmth of his tone and his religious sensitivity. This is an empathetic study with no evidence of a superior or belittling attitude. It is also clearly written without ob-scurantist jargon. Consequently this book will interest you if you are a sociologist of religion, a purveyor or consumer of *Alpha,* or merely a curious onlooker.

PROFESSOR ANDREW WALKER
King's College, London

Introduction

9 to 5 for the next 30 years.
Surely there's more to life.

The *Alpha* course.
Starting soon at a church near you.

This, and other challenging messages, have become a familiar sight in recent years. They have appeared on posters and billboards throughout Britain – from large displays in inner-city areas, to prominent positions on the noticeboards of remote rural parish churches. Leaflets, with similar messages, have dropped through several million letter boxes. Local and national newspapers have also carried other eye-catching invitations and provocative inducements to discover the Christian faith:

Job, flat, car, girlfriend, season ticket to United. Still not satisfied?

You're born. You live. You die. End of story?

An opportunity to explore the meaning to life.

Christianity: Boring, untrue and irrelevant?

This near-saturation advertising campaign spearheaded the so-called 'national initiative' launched at the end of 1998. *Alpha* had arrived in earnest.

The *Alpha* programme is an evangelising campaign that has been endorsed by well over six thousand churches in

Britain and thousands more worldwide. Much heralded in many quarters of Christendom, practically all church traditions and denominations have praised the value of *Alpha* and have come widely to accept it as almost the last word in contemporary evangelism. While *Alpha* has been around for nearly two decades, the 'national initiative' nonetheless put it firmly on the map and considerably raised its public profile.

As the poster advertisements suggest, *Alpha* is based upon a course run at local churches. It does, in fact, amount to a ten-week crash course in Christianity. The rationale is to present the opportunity for the unconverted to delve into the basics of the faith. In theory, it is administered in a friendly and 'safe' atmosphere – one which encourages debate and exploration. Its wider agenda is to win converts in an age of disbelief, religious pluralism and the demise of the nation's principal religion. The ultimate aim is, therefore, to reverse the decline in church attendance which is now at an all-time low.

For a sociologist of religion, which is my professional vocation, *Alpha* is of particular interest. It is innovatory. For one thing, *Alpha* appears to advance what is, in some respects, a distinctive form of Christianity. It brings a popularised expression of the faith, which is shaped considerably by the charismatic movement that has expanded its influence in Britain for nearly four decades and, on a global level, constitutes the fastest spreading strand of the Christian Church. *Alpha* also musters a great deal of what has been learned by the Church over a number of years, or at least its evangelical wing, about how to spread the 'good news'. Hence, it utilises techniques which are very much state-of-the-art: applied sociology, psychology, business and organisational theory. For these reasons it has met with mixed receptions, causing much rejoicing and not a little controversy.

Alpha is of great interest for other reasons besides. This books considers a number of them. It explores the background and working philosophy of *Alpha* and asks the following questions. Who put it together and why? What *kind* of Christianity is being advanced? What does its working philosophy tell us about the changes which have recently taken place within the Christian Church? The following chapters also attempt to find out what kind of people sign up for an *Alpha* course, what initially attracts them, and what their experiences are. More widely, it explores how *Alpha* works on the ground – in the local church. Then there are perhaps the ultimate questions to be addressed. Does *Alpha* work? Is it winning converts? Does it transform people's lives – or at least set them on a spiritual road, as it professes to do?

I would argue that whether *Alpha* works or not is of considerable significance since it provides a measurement of the condition of Christianity today. Firstly, as an evangelising technique it is probably the best that the contemporary Church presently has to offer in an attempt to win converts. Secondly, if it fails to succeed in its aims, then it might be argued that allegiance to Christianity will continue its long-term decline – one which is unlikely to be reversed at the beginning of a new century in an increasingly secular society. Alternatively, it might tap a latent spirituality, especially among those who have never known church life and are coming across the gospel message for the first time. If so, it may be that a religious revival is just around the corner.

In this book I will attempt to answer some of the pertinent questions by making observations based upon fieldwork research. For an eighteen-month period, extending from 1998 through to 1999, I interviewed a number of clergymen and church leaders running *Alpha* at the local level as well as several dozen individuals who had enrolled for the course and asked them, and some 400 other lay people, to fill in questionnaires. I also experienced *Alpha* first hand, having sat in on a number of courses in churches from different denominations. Here then, are some of the findings of the survey and broader observations of the largest and most influential evangelising endeavour of recent times.

My approach in this book is sociological rather than theological. It is written by an agnostic outsider, but one who has a reasonable grasp of theology and a love of church history. Hopefully, this is all brought to bear in a constructive and sensitive overview of *Alpha*. In many regards there is not the space entirely to do justice to the topic, given its scope. Hence, the observations made here are inevitably limited and, subsequently, the conclusions reached are rather tentative. Nonetheless, I think that there is sufficient material to make some constructive comments now that *Alpha* has been launched nationwide, indeed worldwide.

Finally, a few acknowledgements. I am grateful to those earnest and dedicated people who have participated in this study – often with frank and discerning comments about the *Alpha* programme which they have participated in as either an organiser or a 'guest'. Likewise, I am indebted to those involved in *Alpha* who have made constructive comments about the early drafts of this book. I am also grateful to my research assistant, Nikki Lightly, for conducting a number of the interviews and for undertaking the arduous task of proof reading this text. I hope the book is of interest and practical use to members of the Christian community – whatever their theological, ecclesiastical and cultural persuasions. I do not assume a great deal of prior knowledge about *Alpha* from the reader. This could be an advantage or a disadvantage of the book. At the very least, I hope that it generates some positive discussion.

Chapter 1

'Alpha: I've Heard of That!'

The scale of Alpha

In early 1999, I gave my first talk on the subject of Alpha to the Sociology Department at the University of Reading. The audience consisted of a mixture of academics, students and members of the university's chaplaincy who sat excitedly at the front of the gathering. I began by asking whether anyone had ever heard of Alpha. To my dismay only three out of the forty or so assembled had – these being the clergy from the chaplaincy. It was a timely reminder that what is of interest to a sociologist of religion may be irrelevant to the great bulk of the population. The fact that only a few in the audience had heard of Alpha may also be indicative of its level of success in Britain. However, academics and students far from constitute a representative sample of people. Neither, for that matter, do clergy.

A MORI opinion poll, conducted between June and September 1999, indicated that in the 'real' world a somewhat larger proportion of the population had come across Alpha and displayed at least a vague idea of what it was all about. The poll revealed that around 11 per cent recognised the Alpha logo of the figure of a man struggling to carry a question mark almost his own size (presumably symbolising the meaning of life). About 9 per cent who had heard of Alpha understood that it was a Christian evangelistic programme and, of these, about two-thirds had personally enrolled or knew someone who had. *Alpha*, it appeared, had made at least some impact.

Perhaps there is no excuse for not having heard of *Alpha*. British churches have certainly tried sufficiently hard to promote it and sustain a high profile for several years. In September 1998, over 4000 churches (all supposedly contributing £100 to the campaign) of all denominations came together at London's Docklands Arena to launch the £1 million initiative. In the weeks which followed, more than 1700 large billboards were posted nationwide, while smaller posters were pinned up on church noticeboards. All in all, approximately 5500 poster sites were set up. Advertisements were placed in 850 local newspapers across the country, in addition to those in several national newspapers.[1] Free nationwide publicity was also given to the campaign by major television and radio stations in Britain. ITV's flagship news programme *News at Ten* carried the *Alpha* national initiative as a major news item, while BBC1 devoted an entire edition of *Songs of Praise* to its launch. The message via all these forms of media was clear: to encourage people 'to explore the meaning of life' through the Christian faith in a fresh and innovating way.

The posters were meant to be the most prominent part of the campaign. Those who had run *Alpha* for some time had learned through experience that people largely joined a course as a result of personal contacts – friends, relatives, neighbours and work associates. This meant that a rather limited section of the population was being reached with the gospel message and that those who knew of *Alpha* did so mostly through association with people already in the churches. The national initiative of *Alpha* therefore marked an attempt to move away from personal contacts, as valued as they were, to saturation advertising, in order to reach those previously untouched. The poster campaign epitomised the fresh strategy and also indicated a new way of thinking about communicating with the public. The posters did not

include quotations of biblical text. There was no call to repentance or denunciation of sin. In short, there was little to put
people off. The posters, then, were deliberately designed to be
eye-catching, challenging but not intrusive, and tended to
be zany. In support of the rather vague messages the posters
carried, every house in Britain was meant to have been
leafleted – many of these leaflets carrying contact addresses.
Although 4.5 million leaflets were distributed, this did not
quite come off. Neither was there any contact address displayed on the large billboards. 'The *Alpha* course. Starting at
a church near you' was as close as things got to specifics.
The initiative, then, appeared to lay with the 'customer' – the
religious 'seeker'.

A team of five Christians from the advertising industry gave
their free time to design the posters. One of them was Francis
Goodwin, the managing director of the firm Maiden Outdoor,
which operates its own poster sites. Goodwin claimed that:

> We wanted people to feel that an *Alpha* course is a
> perfectly normal thing to do . . . We needed to establish
> the *Alpha* name in the world outside the church
> community and to link its logo with the name, thus
> helping create a brand image. We chose posters to give
> the campaign an impact at street level and to
> communicate with a large audience.[2]

Previously, the design of contemporary Christian posters had
got the advertising team behind *Alpha* into more than a little
hot water. It was they who had designed the much derided
Christmas 1996 poster for the Churches Advertising
Network, which proclaimed: 'Bad hair day? You're a virgin,
you've just given birth and now three kings have shown up.'
Alpha posters were a little less controversial but no less
striking.

Early days

Why was such a large-scale campaign launched in late 1998? In order to answer this question, and to have a broad understanding of *Alpha*, we need to locate it within the context of earlier developments. The national initiative was hailed by many church leaders as perhaps the most significant development of the so-called 'Decade of Evangelism', which marked a large-scale and long-term evangelising effort by British churches. The Decade of Evangelism was launched with vast optimism in 1990 and came to have considerable symbolic and psychological significance for many Christians. As its designation suggests, the 1990s was heralded as a decade in which various evangelising campaigns would be used to spread the Christian faith. *Alpha* can be seen, then, as the latest and largest of a number of initiatives embarked upon by many of the more evangelical-minded churches in order to reinvigorate the faith and fill church pews. For this reason *Alpha* was fully endorsed by the Evangelical Alliance – the umbrella organisation for the majority of evangelical (mostly charismatic) churches in Britain.

Alpha followed a number of other rather unsuccessful evangelising initiatives in the early/mid-1990s (also largely based on leafleting and poster campaigns). Two of the most significant were *Minus to Plus* – the title of which clearly recognised church attendance decline – and *Jesus in Me* (JIM), launched by the Pentecostal denominations Elim and the Assemblies of God. The failure of such campaigns was epitomised by the latter which aimed at winning 250,000 converts but, in the event, achieved only 20,000, of which many were believed to be those returning to the faith rather than discovering it for the first time. More broadly, the muted success of these proselytising initiatives appeared to exemplify the abject failure of the much proclaimed Decade of Evangelism.

By contrast, at least measured by the number of churches

involved, the initial developments of the *Alpha* national initiative looked promising. This certainly appeared to be so at the end of 1998 and the early part of 1999. Other churches began to join the *Alpha* bandwagon and as they did so the ecumenical endeavour strengthened the relationship between them. This was not least of all in respect of the Roman Catholic Church and the range of Protestant denominations which continue to work together in campaigning and propagating local initiatives. At the end of 1998 some 6,300 churches in Britain were registered to run the course.[3] This apparent increasing interest by British churches, however, was part of long-term developments. Nationally, the use of *Alpha* had slowly spread over a period of 5–10 years. 1995 proved to be a watershed in its expanding popularity as the programme went countrywide for the first time. The so-called 'national initiative' of 1998 was aimed at bringing *Alpha* to saturation point in order to enhance its public profile.

Year	Number of churches running Alpha[4]
1991	4
1992	5
1993	200
1994	740
1995	2,500
1996	5,000
1997	6,700
1998	10,500

Within weeks of the launch of the national campaign, *Alpha* had 'gone global' to reach over 75 countries. By mid 1999, its organisers claimed that there were 11,430 *Alpha* courses up and running globally, including those set up by some 6500 churches in Britain. In total, so it was asserted, over one million people across the world had been through the course since 1995.[5] Outside of Britain, numerous *Alpha* programmes had been established in Europe, including Albania, Romania and other ex-communist countries. Hundreds more were set up in the USA, with the Association of Vineyard Churches being the major initiator. Such far-flung places as Australia, Russia and countries in Latin America and the Far East, and sometimes more remote parts of the world, also found a home for *Alpha*. Another sign of its international dimension is that the *Alpha* course booklet and other accompanying literature has been published in at least 17 languages. Moreover, *Alpha*, it seemed, was not only international but, as in Britain, ecumenical, drawing together Protestants, Roman Catholics and Orthodox Christians from all over the world in a number of interlocking networks.

Britain, however, remained the hub of *Alpha* activities. Between March and July in 1998 alone, there were 19 major international and 6 regional conferences held in different parts of the country. *Alpha*, so it is boasted by its organisers, is now run in 120 British jails and other penal institutions to the apparent delight of prison governors and the Home Secretary![6] An *Alpha* worldwide website has also been created which claimed to have received over 17,000 international 'visitors' by June 1998. Based in Britain, *Alpha* has also grown into a highly commercialised international industry which has helped generate a kind of Christian sub-culture all of its own. There are copious amounts of accompanying audio and visual cassettes and literature, much of which can be purchased at local Christian bookshops. Some books have been veritable best-sellers. These include *Questions of Life* (retailing at £5.99) which is believed to have sold nearly 200,000 copies. There are also *Alpha* brochures, a poster pack, sweatshirts and car stickers, and not to mention the *Alpha Cookbook*.

Why *Alpha*?

Alpha bills itself as 'a ten week practical introduction to the Christian faith': it is apparently designed to present the principles of the Christian faith to the inquisitive in a relaxed and informal setting. As will be more fully documented in the next chapter, it is the brainchild of the large Anglican church, Holy Trinity, Brompton. In the long term, Holy Trinity, and other churches which support its venture, seek to win converts. In the short term, the aim of *Alpha* is to set people on a spiritual road, or at least to get them to begin to think about what Christianity has to offer. To put it succinctly, according to Ben Pollard (a pastoral adviser to Nicky Gumbel who heads the initiative at Holy Trinity), whom I interviewed shortly after the launch of the national initiative, '*Alpha* is about winning converts, but even more it provides a basic introduction to Christianity through a neighbourhood awareness campaign'.[7] The rationale behind *Alpha*, and the way that it has been devised, surely marks a recognition that we live in a secular society and that the Christian Church has been on the decline in Britain and other countries in the West for many years (the USA being something of an exception). Britain is indeed a very good example. It may be more secular than the USA, and perhaps less so than some Scandinavian countries. Nevertheless, there is no getting away from the fact that Britain's historically dominant faith, Christianity, is on the downturn and has been so for decades. British society and its institutions, political and educational among them, have disengaged themselves from the faith. Political and moral debates are rarely couched in religious terms. The pronouncements of established Christian church leaders carry little weight. At the same time Britain is also an increasingly pluralist society. In terms of competing religions, this means that Christianity is now rivalled by the faiths of ethnic minorities (there are over one million practising Muslims and 400,000 Hindus in Britain), as well as the growth of a host of New Religious Movements, the New Age and so on.

There are also other indications of the demise of Christianity. A principal one is religious observance. Much is epitomised by the passing of the Christian Sabbath. In a materialist society there are now numerous alternatives to the traditional Christian Sunday – garden centres, DIY, major sporting events, and much, much more besides. Then there is perhaps the ultimate indicator of the health of Christianity in Britain – the decline of church attendance and membership, to which *Alpha* largely addresses itself. Let us look briefly at some of the evidence. Clearly, there has been a long-term downward spiral of church attendance, as indicated in the various 'Censuses of Religion', commencing in 1851. In that year, just under 40 per cent of the population of England and Wales attended church on a Sunday, with the figure falling to 35 per cent by the turn of the century and 20 per cent in 1950. This was followed by a spectacular decline throughout the 1960s as attendance figures dropped to around 15 per cent.[8]

In the last two decades there have been few substantial surveys of church attendance and membership in Britain. The most significant is probably the 1989 Church Census, which, however, is limited solely to England rather than all parts of Britain. The findings were published in *Christian England.*[9] It revealed that, between 1975 and 1979, church attendance dropped by 2 per cent – from 4.2 million to 4 million – and in the subsequent decade there was a further drop to 3.7 million.[10] In 1989, only approximately 9.5 per cent of the population attended a church on Sunday.[11] No denomination escaped the observable downward trend. During the period 1975–89 there was a spectacular fall in attendance at Roman Catholic and Anglican churches, as well as the larger non-conformist denominations such as the Baptists, Methodists and the United Reformed Church. There was also a significant reversal of attendance among the smaller Christian fellowships including the Salvation Army, Quakers, Lutheran churches, and Seventh-Day Adventists.[12]

We must of course be wary of statistics. Those related to the attendance of religious institutions in themselves may not tell us everything about the strength of Christianity in Britain, or indeed, any other form of religiosity. After all, some academics have been more optimistic and identified a widespread 'believing without belonging'. In short, there is indication of a high degree of 'hidden' religious belief in more individualistic and privatised forms. It is just that in contemporary society people are not attracted to institutionalised religion.[13] This is part of a broader social trend. As Grace Davie has explained, in her survey of religion in Britain in the early 1990s, individualistic cultural tendencies invariably undermine the necessity to belong to any form of voluntary association, whether religious or secular – trade unions, sports clubs, knitting circles, the Church. Davie, however, argued that while there was an apparent decline in belonging, there was also a parallel demise in believing. This was particularly the case with the young: 'Not only have the young left our churches, they are, it seems, rejecting even nominal belief.'[14]

The signs, then, are surely unmistakable. The trend for well over a century in Britain is that Christianity is suffering a serious long-term slump. It is probable that this decline is irreversible. However, let us assume for a moment that it is not and that there may well be many people who are searching for a meaningful and relevant faith. It could be that the churches of today are not an appealing proposition or that they have failed to advance the faith in an attractive and significant way. *Alpha* may therefore feasibly provide an opportunity to engage with some of these current relevant debates. Above all, it could plausibly provide a measurement, albeit a rather crude one, of the level of religious seekership which exists in British society and whether Christianity presents a viable proposition. It offers the chance to find out, as the poster suggests, whether or not Christianity really is 'Boring, Untrue and Irrelevant'.

The view of many leading churchmen is that there is a latent spirituality which can be tapped. Much of this has been shown by the words of the Archbishop of Canterbury, Dr George Carey. Strongly supporting the growth of the *Alpha* programme, he applauded the plans for the national advertising initiative in 1998 and spelt out some of the difficulties facing the contemporary Church:

> Many young people today have no experience of church. We have seen the country moving through materialism. Sometimes there has been exploration into the New Age movement or whatever. A lot of people are saying, 'These things didn't satisfy. I wonder if there may be something in historic, orthodox Christianity.' Churches are growing significantly as a result of people coming to a personal faith in Christ through one of these [*Alpha*] courses.[15]

New directions

Some evangelical Christians may speak nostalgically of the large-scale proselytising campaigns of the 1950s and early 1960s, typified by those fronted by American evangelist Billy Graham. But gone are the days when such campaigns could attract tens of thousands of people at large arenas or similar venues. Those of the controversial American healing evangelist Morris Cerullo, and one or two others who have a particular appeal to the African and Afro-Caribbean communities in Britain, are very much an exception. Social change in the form of individual and privatised lifestyles means that even fewer people are attracted to such large public events. This is indicative of wider developments. After all, attendances at soccer matches, whatever the hype, are not what they used to be. Evangelism had therefore come to

require a totally new direction – a more personal one. Moreover, it had to present a soft, not a hard sell. Put more
directly, a fresh approach to evangelism, typified by *Alpha*,
needed to be one which was user-friendly. There was no room
for 'in your face', repent or to hell with you, obtrusive Christianity. The working philosophy has been to ease people into
the faith in their own time, pace and at their leisure. It was
necessary too to be relevant. After all, Jesus attempted to be
relevant to those of his own time. This was what the parables
were supposed to be all about.

Alpha, then, claims to take people on their own terms,
but in doing so addresses the profound need to establish a
package of Christianity which bridges the ever widening gulf
between Church and secular culture. Partly, this was
because, in an age of unbelief, Church and secular culture
had long gone their separate ways. Hence, the church
environment had become a distant and alienated one for
many people. For most, weddings and funerals were likely to
be as near as they got to church attendance during their
entire lives. Partly, too, the problem was one generated by the
churches themselves in that they frequently seemed, at least
to outsiders, to offer little more than a dry, ritualised and
spiritless Christianity. Many of the dilemmas have been
summed up by Sandy Millar from Holy Trinity, Brompton,
one of the key movers in the *Alpha* programme, who has
maintained that a demand is still very much 'out there'. The
problem, however, was in the Church reaching people. As he
has argued, with a tone of abundant optimism:

> Questions about God have fascinated human beings
> since time began. Many men and women today
> experience a very real sense of spiritual hunger without
> having any contact with a church.
>
> One of the most frustrating aspects of church life,
> until recently, has been our ineffectiveness in reaching
> people with this hunger and getting them within the

sound of the gospel. We have longed to find a way of
enabling them to discover the liberating, life-changing
power of God, revealed in His Son Jesus Christ through
his Holy Spirit, in a way that allows them to explore in
an unthreatening atmosphere of love and acceptance.
Until recently they have been hard to interest.[16]

The question was, could *Alpha* make a difference?

Chapter 2

The Background to *Alpha*

Welcome to HTB

To appreciate fully the *Alpha* initiative and what its chief aims are, it is imperative to know more about the historical background against which it was devised and subsequently evolved. Here, a consideration of the role of the well-known Anglican charismatic church, Holy Trinity, Brompton, is indispensable. HTB, as it is affectionately known, may not sound anything particularly noteworthy. Indeed, in terms of architecture it is, from the outside at least, an inconspicuous-looking inner-London parish church. It is to be found tucked away behind the far grander Roman Catholic Oratory of St Philip Neri, next to the Victoria and Albert Museum in Kensington. Its modest structure, however, belies its national, indeed international, importance in evangelical circles.

HTB is the wealthiest parish church in Britain, with an annual income of around £2.3 million. Perhaps this is not too surprising given the impressive size of its congregation and the fact that its immediate parishioners are drawn from the affluent community near Harrods and Kensington High Street. However, there are also many other sources of income, including the commercial industry that has built up around *Alpha*, which has helped to make HTB one of the most influential churches in Britain. In fact, it has grown to enjoy a global significance since the church had become, even before the 1998 *Alpha* initiative, the headquarters of an evangelical movement stretching with an elaborate system of church networks from Argentina to New Zealand.

The rather dowdy exterior of HTB hides an impressive interior of well-furnished conference rooms and a basement coffee shop. There is also a bookshop which stocks the full range of *Alpha* paraphernalia, including an impressive array of Christian literature and teaching material, as well as the compact discs and audio and video tapes that have become a familiar part of the contemporary Christian scene. All in all, HTB is positively worth a visit. It is a busy and bustling church which never closes – there is always something going on. In no uncertain terms, HTB is the centre of what can rightly be described as the *Alpha* 'movement'. Those interested in running *Alpha* can embark on training courses at the church, while teams of HTB representatives will attend a local church, if requested, to explain exactly what *Alpha* entails. HTB is also the centre for both national and international conferences which have *Alpha* as their theme.

A look around the elaborate decoration of the main part of the church gives away the fact that Holy Trinity was once of High Church tradition. However, like other churches of its ilk, most of the visual clues to its former allegiances are now hidden by all the trappings of contemporary worship – drums, guitars and the screens upon which lyrics of up-to-date Christian songs are projected during services. Fading religious pictures and the altar are almost obscured. While traditionalists might be, at best, saddened by such developments, there is no denying the fact that HTB is a highly successful church, with near on two thousand people attending its services on a Sunday. It presents itself, not surprisingly, as a role-model for others who might wish to emulate its accomplishments. At the same time there is no escaping the fact that HTB is thoroughly charismatic, both theologically and culturally, in its orientation. This is important because of the repercussions this has for the underlying philosophy of the *Alpha* course and its content.

In short, this means that HTB and its *Alpha* courses have been inspired by ideas and programmes which the wider charismatic movement has embraced for a number of years. These influences deserve some consideration.

Influences on *Alpha*

There is nothing particularly new about *Alpha*, certainly in some of its key aims. The so-called *Life in the Spirit* course was initiated by churches involved in the charismatic renewal movement in 1972. Like *Alpha*, it used personal networks to try to integrate people into church culture and, ultimately, to win them over by the exploration of the Christian faith. One of the repercussions was that it helped to spread the beliefs and practices of the charismatic movement through British churches. And, as I will argue below, this may also have become one of the principal functions of *Alpha*.

More recently, the independent, so-called New Churches have taken a similar approach to *Alpha* and, in many instances, have run courses which predate it. For instance, Gerald Coates' Pioneers, based in the affluent suburbs of west Surrey, have run 'Focus Groups' along much the same lines as *Alpha* for several years. In many of the churches of the older denominations, such strategies were increasingly looked upon with admiration and not infrequently imitated. However, to these mainline churches *Alpha* appeared to be the most promising way forward. In turn, HTB has continually refined and modified *Alpha*, taking into account many of the requirements and comments of these churches in order to perfect the programme and to make it more appealing than any rival. What, then, are the advantages of *Alpha*? And, what does it have that the other initiatives did not?

Perhaps the principal attraction of *Alpha* is that it explicitly sets out not to pressurise. People who are interested are encouraged not to sign up for an entire course, but only for one week at a time. If they drop out they are not, in theory at least, contacted and coerced into rejoining. Those who do enlist are eased into the course and generally only after the first few weeks are the so-called 'searching issues', the major means of exploring Christianity, addressed in earnest. This softly-softly approach, however, is only one alluring aspect of *Alpha.*

Another appeal of the programme is its aim to put the needs of the 'customer' first. The principal rationale behind the initiative is to encourage people to raise issues about the Christian faith. For this reason Holy Trinity has spent several years finding out what matters and interests people, what kinds of issues are relevant, and what questions are most frequently asked about Christianity. In previous years questionnaires have been administered to this end. At first the emphasis was on how people questioned issues specifically related to the main Christian topics of faith, such as the mystery of the Trinity or the divinity of Christ. This was then broadened to take in controversial topics, such as sexuality, suffering and the apparent contradiction between science and faith.

Although the refined *Alpha* course, which is at the core of the national initiative, has its own history, it has also been influenced by various sources. Most of these are earlier evangelical strategies which helped forge *Alpha* into what it is today. Some of the most significant have had an impact over three decades or more – especially in charismatic circles and for very distinct reasons. When examined, it is clear that these earlier initiatives are particularly noteworthy because they have significant bearing on ideas about winning converts through networking and by crossing church–secular divides.

The first influence upon *Alpha* was the so-called 'homogeneous unit principle', which had, for several years, come to underpin popular strategies of church growth. In short, the homogeneous unit principle means that 'like attracts like'. People are most likely to be won over to a church constituted by people similar to themselves. This kind of idea can be traced back to the pioneering work of Donald McGavran at Fuller Seminary in the USA. McGavran believed that in bringing about church growth in the West, much could be learned from the years of experience of missionaries in the Third World. In countries such as India, it was difficult to make individual converts because people were part of well-established communities with their own long-held values and traditions. To a lesser extent this was also true in the West. People therefore had to be lured out of their former social allegiances and into new (Christian) ones. However, this transition could be eased if evangelism was conducted through social networks of people with similar backgrounds.

This type of theorising was developed into something of a science at Fuller by Peter Wagner who argued that entire congregations could be built through effective networking of people with similar life experiences, background and outlook. There was, however, more to the equation. For Wagner, evangelism also had to be relevant and made applicable to different cultural contexts. The roots of this theorising can be traced back to the philosophies of church-growth strategies that had developed at Fuller at several decades.

The secret of successful evangelism, for many of the strategists at Fuller, was that it was necessary to be pertinent to present-day society. Concessions could be made to contemporary culture, while advancing a form of Christianity that clung to the fundamentals of the faith – relevance without compromise. As an early founder of the 'church-growth' school, Wagner also argued that the best way of 'making disciples of all nations', as commanded by Christ, was to use secular methods of business and organisational growth, alongside the insights presented by sociology and psychology. This working philosophy was later elaborated by yet another product of Fuller, the late healing evangelist John Wimber, who was to go on to have considerable impact upon the charismatic scene in Britain, and indeed globally, throughout the 1980s and early 1990s.[1]

Wimber was invited to Britain by a handful of influential Anglican charismatic Christians in the early 1980s. His teachings spread rapidly to the extent that something of a theological and pastoral revolution took place in many British charismatic churches, alongside the increasing acceptance of his distinctive proselytising tactics. Some of Wimber's teachings, at least those which developed the homogeneous unit principle, appeared to be sociologically sound. In the past, people were socialised into church life, or what might be described as an 'ascribed' religious status. To put it succinctly, there was once the tendency for people to grow up in particular churches and denominations. The primary reason for attending the village Anglican church or local Baptist chapel was because one's parents or neighbours did so. Today the basis of belonging is different and this recognition was part and parcel of Wimber's teachings on church growth. In the contemporary world, where there is a great deal more social and geographical mobility, people gravitate towards churches comprised of people like themselves and establish an 'achieved' religious status as a matter of choice rather than as a result of social pressures. Wimber also recognised that significant social networks and interpersonal bonds are the *means* by which people belong. Again, this has a great deal of sociological credence and has been proven by academic studies before and since Wimber appeared on the scene.[2]

Alpha marks an explicit recognition of the viability of such church-growth strategies and the profound social changes which have taken place over the last few decades. This is certainly true of the notion that 'like attracts like'. The contemporary world has various sources of identity and the focal points of social belonging are complex. Age, ethnic origins and gender are important, besides social class. This recognition has been exploited in church circles and is the basis of congregational growth for many of the largest and most successful churches in Britain. For instance, Kensington Temple, the flagship of the Elim Pentecostal Church, not a million miles from HTB, has dozens of satellite churches constructed on the basis of different ethnic communities.

Likewise, the organisers of *Alpha* have taken the significance of social networks seriously and have, as part of a wider strategy, targeted particular social groups. Hence, HTB has deliberately devised its own course for the people using the like-attracts-like principle as a source of church growth and to win over the next generation. Youth clubs and schools around the world are busily running the *Youth Alpha* course, with its own specially designed manuals aimed at two age groups: the 11–14s and 15–18s. While the syllabus is the same as the main *Alpha* programme, it is especially refined for young people. Also used is the book *Questions of Life* and other distinctive training manuals which give guidelines on how to communicate the course to youngsters. In addition, *Student Alpha* appeals to its own clientele and, similarly, the course has been customised for the needs of students in higher education. Then there is *Daytime Alpha*, first run at HTB, which is directed at other distinct social groups – those who are most likely to be free during the day to attend the course, such as young mothers, women's groups, the unemployed, elderly people and shift workers.

Complementing the impact of the homogeneous unit principle and the recognition of social networks has been the influence of the more recent so-called church 'cell revolution'. The invention, or at least the major inspiration, sprang from the Faith Community Baptist Church in Singapore in the 1990s. The cell revolution is based upon business strategies and the FCBC claims to have won over hundreds of thousands of converts worldwide by utilising these strategies. This church-growth scheme, broadly speaking, is built upon the recognition that most churches have two aspects that make up their social dynamics. The first is the congregation which meets on a Sunday for worship – where people briefly interact and then disperse. Here, there is little meaningful sustained contact. The second is a host of small-scale networks and organisations which are the real essence of church life – women's circles, boy scout groups, youth groups, and so on. These are the rough parallels to 'cells'. The idea is to abolish all other groups and sub-divide the church into cells comprised of about a dozen people, each one with a leader. This is a tightly knit group based on locality and, more often than not, similar social composition or pre-existing networks.

The ultimate aim of the cell revolution is to win converts through networking with similar people and 'significant others', whether neighbours, work associates or school friends. When the cell becomes too big, in theory by co-opting converts, it sub-divides and the process is carried on. To some extent *Alpha* works along the same principles. This is not to over-emphasise the impact of the cell revolution. There is evidence that some churches of different denominations in Britain have been busy dispersing their girl guides and men's fellowships and have replaced them with cells. In the long term it is likely that in Britain this will all turn out to be something of a fad. However, it does emphasise how the notion of networking with significant others is accepted as one of the principal keys to successful evangelising.

Yet another influence on the development of the *Alpha* programme is the renowned church growth strategy of the Willow Creek Community Church in Illinois, USA. A successful fellowship with thousands of members, it claims to have the secret of bridging church and secular culture. For Willow Creek it is imperative to allow people to feel comfortable with Christianity and the Church as an institution. Being comfortable is not limited to avoiding frightful ideas such as hell and eternal damnation. It is the promise of heaven and what Christianity can do for the believer in the here and now which enjoys the greater emphasis. Furthermore, church life, according to Willow Creek, should be

intimate, safe and friendly. It should be as familiar and wel-
coming as a person's home environment. In turn, this kind
of thinking has led to *Alpha* courses usually being held at
someone's house rather than the alienating environment of
the local church. Hence, the potential convert is, at least in
theory, eased into church culture over a period of time.

The Willow Creek church has also developed what has come
to be known as 'Seeker Services'. These are distinct from the
'Believers' Services' for those who have graduated to full-
blown Christianity and accompanying church culture. Some
of these varied services are held in mid-week to move away
from the traditional Christian Sunday and all that it entails.
In addition, the church has different evangelising ministries
to interact with people at different stages of spiritual development and different social backgrounds. Then there are the
church's shopping malls which symbolise the attempt to
integrate the necessities of modern consumer life with
church attendance in a practical way.

The church-growth strategies of Willow Creek and other
agencies discussed above have proved to be particularly
popular with the more evangelical, explicitly charismatic
churches in Britain. This is hardly surprising given that the
charismatic movement has always carried with it, from the
mid-1960s onwards, the hope of revival. In short, there has
long been a preoccupation with the mass winning of converts
and the attempt to bring what was often envisaged as a
deeper and 'truer' expression of Christianity. Although the
exclusivism once associated with the movement is now not
so apparent, a conviction that a revival in terms of church
growth is just around the corner remains imperative and has
ensured that *Alpha* is a mainstay of evangelising initiatives.

The contemporary charismatic movement
At this point more needs to be said about the relationship of
Alpha with the wider charismatic movement even if this

means conducting something of a brief historical detour – especially for those readers with little knowledge of the significance of the movement in Britain and, more broadly, on a global scale.[3] Indeed, in appreciating the significance of *Alpha*, such an understanding of the background of the movement is not only useful but imperative.

The charismatic movement of today has its origins in the 1960s, although its roots are deeper and can be traced back to the beginning of the twentieth century and even earlier. The movement is otherwise known as neo-Pentecostalism. This designation implies that it is a new version of an older religious manifestation. The earlier Pentecostal movement, with its legendary beginnings at the Azusa Street mission in San Francisco in 1906, and its counterpart in Britain during the Welsh Revival, is now typically referred to as 'classical' Pentecostalism. Like its predecessor, and earlier revivals in the nineteenth century on both sides of the Atlantic, the charismatic movement challenged what it perceived as the spiritual deadness of the churches and what appeared to be increasing secularity and unbelief in wider society.

Part of the mission was to reverse the observable decline in church attendance. Like the previous renewal movements, the mid-century charismatic movement, in both Roman Catholic and Protestant Churches, advocated a return to the pristine spiritual condition of the first-century Church in order to reverse decline. For those involved in the movement this meant a spiritual renewal and experience of the charismata (glossolalia or gift of tongues, prophecy, healing, etc.) and for whom the terms 'revival', 'awakening', or the 'outpouring of the Holy Spirit' were frequently used to designate a return to the pentecostal experiences of early Christianity.

Today, the scale of Pentecostalism is impressive. With some justification, Peter Wagner has argued that on a global level Pentecostalism is the most significant non-political and non-military social movement for over half a century.[4] Nonetheless, this has been less the case in the West, certainly in

Britain. While the charismatic movement could boast a measure of success, this is to be evaluated in relative terms. The evidence suggests that many charismatic churches, denominational and independent, are at least holding their own in terms of church membership compared to their non-charismatic cousins.[5] It is clear, however, that the charismatic movement has failed to reverse long-term church decline. Moreover, it is evident that not only has the movement largely failed to substantially rejuvenate the churches as a whole, but that it has now been reduced to a largely stagnant enclave in a slowly but surely declining Christian constituency.

As it began to flounder by the late 1970s, the renewal movement fairly rapidly diluted some of its principal elements. The controversial emphasis on the charismata and the 'Baptism in the Spirit' were no longer regarded as the necessary distinguishing characteristics of the 'born-again' Christian. While this can be attributed to the relentless process of what the sociologist Max Weber once called 'the routinisation of charisma' (an inevitable spiritual dampening of a religious movement over generations),[6] its watering down was also in order to widen its appeal and, in essence, increase its 'marketability'. By the 1980s, the cultural and liturgical trappings of renewal had spread widely through the established churches, but very often the substance and principal teachings, and the charismata, were not to be observed. This is an important consideration. While it appears that the charismatic movement has continued to spread throughout British churches – and, as I will argue below, this is important in the *Alpha* context – the movement is not the same one that emerged in the 1960s. It has been transformed, modified and, in some regards, compromised.

Another indication of the decline in the tendency towards exclusiveness by contemporary Pentecostals are the developments within the 'New Churches', such as New Frontiers, Team Spirit, Ichthus and the Pioneers.[7] These churches have evolved from their more sectarian origins in the earlier so-called Restorationist movement, which may itself have even outdated the emergence of the Renewal movement in the mainline churches. As they began to decline (in terms of membership) from the mid 1980s, the New Churches became far more open to wider cultural developments and came to see themselves as partners with charismatics from the mainline denominations. Many became particularly apt in marketing the faith and developed a distinct form of state-of-the-art, rather commercialised Christian sub-culture. Indeed, there was much in evidence to suggest that they were becoming what Harvey Cox calls 'designer churches', that wished to be judged by the speed of growth of their congregations, funds available, attractive buildings and other hallmarks of success that reflected the wider enterprise culture of the 1980s and 1990s.[8] In turn, the New Churches came to have a considerable influence, culturally and theologically, on the wider Christian scene, primarily through the annual Spring Harvest conventions.

Alpha in many respects epitomises the church-growth imperative of the New Churches and their increasing tendency towards mass-marketing, and the commercial mobilisation of the charismatic movement as a whole. The *Alpha* movement has also expressed a new-found unity in that it has been embraced by churches of practically all persuasions – Roman Catholic, Anglican, the Free Church denominations, and the New Churches, as well as other independent fellowships. By no means are all of them charismatic in orientation but, to one degree or another, many are. The significance of this is that, given the numbers of churches involved, the extensive use of *Alpha* is, to some extent at least, a measurement of the impact and spread of charismatic Christianity.

There is no doubting that Holy Trinity, Brompton, is a charismatic church. Indeed, HTB is one of the 'mega' charismatic churches in Britain and numbers among a network of highly influential churches that have grown up in the last twenty years or so. Prominent leaders at HTB, including Sandy Millar and Nicky Gumbel, are well-known figures within the movement, both nationally and internationally. Included in this influential circle are the leaderships of other large denominational charismatic churches, that of the New Churches, and the Elim Pentecostal church Kensington Temple. In an ever contracting Christian world, this group of personalities have enjoyed considerable status in Britain for well over a decade and have come to establish close relationships with their opposite numbers on an international scale, especially North America – perhaps most significantly with the Association of Vineyard Churches which was established by John Wimber.

Wimber is a key figure in the development of the charismatic movement since the 1980s in Britain. He proved to be both a colourful and controversial character until his death in 1998. His ministry ranged from the constructive and laudable sublime, to the truly ridiculous. His healing strategies, especially in the area of emotional healing, have inspired many Christians with a healing ministry, dealing with problems that the mainstream churches did not know how to deal with or preferred to ignore. More generally, his strategies of church growth regalvanised the charismatic movement in Britain that was fast dying on its feet.

Wimber, however, often kept unorthodox company. In the early 1990s, his reputation was damaged by his association with the so-called Kansas City prophets. The key figure here was Paul Cain. There are various accounts of how Wimber and Cain were destined by God to meet up for specific divine purposes. In 1990 the KCP, headed by Cain, ministered in England to a number of key national church leaders at Holy Trinity, Brompton, and, thereafter to conferences in London and Harrogate. Cain prophesied a world revival in October, beginning in London. Allegedly, Wimber brought his entire family over to a meeting in the Dockland's Arena which was meant to signify the revival predicted to spread across the world as possibly the last great move of God.

For over two years little was heard of Wimber who disassociated himself from the KCP and their erroneous prophecies. However, his reputation had been severely damaged and even the emergence of what came to be known as the Toronto Blessing in 1993 failed to revive his profile. Nonetheless, the Vineyard movement that he led for so long continues to inspire charismatics in Britain. His lasting significance probably lies in the unity he brought to New Churches and mainstream charismatic churches. Since Wimber's arrival they came to have far more in common than ever before in terms of broad aims and theological inclinations.

Over the last ten to fifteen years these churches have also tended to be influenced by the vogues and fashions which surround the wider global charismatic movement, such as strategies of emotional healing and deliverance (a kind of 'lesser exorcism'), a belief in demonic territorial spirits (which smacks of pagan animism as much as anything else) and a passing preoccupation with all things prophetic. Such teaching and practices have impacted to one degree or another and have gained fleeting popularity – rather like passing fads. Then there was the not inconsiderable influence of the so-called Toronto Blessing and, given the church networks and connections already established in Britain, it is not surprising that it spread as rapidly as it did. Furthermore, in the context of *Alpha*, the Toronto Blessing needs more than a passing reference.

The Toronto Blessing and all that stuff

Claims of visions and prophecies may be regarded as essential aspects of charismatic church life. Hysterical laughter, barking and other animal noises, shaking, trembling, twitching, probably less so. However, from the early 1990s these were the identifiable characteristics of the Toronto Blessing, which did its rounds not only in the charismatic churches in Britain but in tens of thousands of others on a global scale.[9] The 'Blessing', as it was more popularly known, became associated with distinct forms of ecstatic and esoteric phenomena. The peculiar manifestations temporarily amused or bewildered the British media, with an article in one popular national newspaper posing the question: 'What in God's name is going on?'[10]

The Toronto Blessing had both its observable physical manifestations and its more hidden dimensions. The distinguishing outward features were fits of laughter, apparently spontaneously breaking out among members of congregations during church services, and such laughter, proclaimed a Christian healing magazine reporting on the Toronto Blessing at the time, 'was therapeutic'.[11] Below these external manifestations were said to be frequent deeply meaningful ecstatic religious experiences. To the fore were prophecies, visions of angels and other forms of divine communication. Such phenomena dominated church life for nearly four years.

The churches involved in the Toronto Blessing attempted to give an interpretation to their experiences. Since it came largely to be understood as the preparation for revival, a great deal of emphasis was placed in the charismatic literature of the time on God's call to holiness, the expansion of the spiritual gifts among Christian congregations, and a belief that backsliders were returning to the fold.[12] The principal theme was that the church was being prepared for possibly the greatest revival ever – one that would subsequently lead, according to some interpretations at least, to the Second Coming of Christ. God was healing, cleansing and preparing the Church through the manifestation of his power.

Sociological explanations of the Toronto Blessing have been few and far between. My personal view is that to some extent at least it resulted from the psychological pressures built up by the prolonged hope for revival. This hope was there to be observed from the very beginning of the charismatic movement but was enhanced by the impact of the Association of Vineyard churches under John Wimber.[13] But there was always more to the equation. Philip Richter has argued that it was necessary to take into account the 'supply-side' of the charismatic movement.[14] He argued that there was room for charismatics to invest in a new enterprise for their share of a relatively static religious market, or at least safeguard the gains which had been made in terms of numerical growth within its own circles. There was, claimed Richter, space to give the 'customer' another dimension of the ecstatic market: in other words, the direct, unmediated and unpredictable encounter with God. Richter also argued that it spread extremely rapidly because, for some time, there was a tendency for charismatic churches to forge links with the various streams of the movement. This was indicative of the intrinsic weakness of the charismatic churches in the precarious religious marketplace. The net result was the attractive package of ecstatic manifestations which disseminated itself globally. The means by which this was accomplished was thoroughly contemporary – electronic communications, videos, evangelical magazines and popular paperbacks.

A long-term observer of the charismatic movement, Andrew Walker, also noted the significance of the growing unity of charismatic churches in terms of the 'spiritual marketplace' throughout the last two decades. It is worth quoting him at length. Walker states:

> What I think is of particular interest in the British context is that by 1990 the charismatic scene had become not only a more co-operative movement, but also an increasingly integrated Christian market. A small group of powerful producers were supplying the spiritual (and shopping) needs of large numbers of religious consumers. So much so, that we can usefully

talk of the development of a Protestant charismatic monopoly (Catholic renewalists had little stake in this enterprise economy, except as occasional consumers) . . . [There are] interconnected rings of charismatic influence and somewhat incestuous (wheels within wheels) which had reached religious consumers at significant arenas of consumption throughout the country . . . I am not suggesting, for a moment, that this Christian market was either a total or a planned monopoly. However, its existence partly explains how, when it broke in 1995, the Toronto Blessing was able to spread so quickly . . .[15]

The great majority of 'mega' charismatic churches were involved in the Toronto Blessing – Queen's Road Baptist Church, Wimbledon; St Andrew's, Chorleywood; Holy Trinity, Brompton, and many others. HTB can be said to have been one of the principal 'carriers' of the Toronto Blessing from the Vineyard Airport Fellowship in Canada, where it is often assumed to have begun. In doing so, it definitely helped put HTB on the map. HTB became the focus of both church and secular media attention. At its height, people queued up outside the church all day to experience and witness the Toronto Blessing. HTB church members were given special identity cards so that they were let into the church first to experience the phenomenon.

The Toronto Blessing had run its course by 1998. In retrospect, it would be easy to trivialise what amounted to a profoundly subjective spiritual experience for many people. Since its disappearance, however, the need to explain what it was all about means that its supporters are now inclined (if it is mentioned at all) to interpret it as one of God's periodic blessings on his people, rather than of great eschatological significance. Some have disowned it completely. For the most part it has been forgotten as rapidly as yesterday's news headlines. There has now followed a more measured and

systematic attempt to win converts.[16] Enter the *Alpha* programme. *Alpha*, however, as pointed out in the last chapter,
is not new. It merely became the fresh focus of interest for
many charismatic churches. It gave some people something
to do as hands lay idle after the Toronto Blessing and may
be interpreted, if one wishes to be particularly cynical, as
forcing the expected revival and fulfilling prophecy. It might
be argued, then, that *Alpha*, at least for some, is a way of
dealing with the sense of discord resulting from the unful-
filled expectations of the Toronto Blessing.

The Toronto Blessing had in many ways brought a unity to
which *Alpha* has applied itself. *Alpha* has also followed many
of the contours that it had cleaved out – following networks
established by the principal churches involved. This is not to
overstress the point, however. Not all those churches
adopting *Alpha* would by any means have embraced the
Toronto Blessing or even heard of it. However, I would estimate that practically all that were involved in the Toronto
Blessing would have readily endorsed *Alpha*. Moreover,
whether they know it or not, those subscribing to *Alpha* are,
to some extent, inheritors of the Toronto Blessing or, at the
very least, inspired by those who advanced it.

One thing is for certain. *Alpha* largely marked the end of
the spectacular and esoteric phenomena which had built up
for well over a decade in British charismatic churches. In
this respect many roads had led to John Wimber. Again
inspired by Peter Wagner, Wimber had taught the significance of 'signs and wonders' or 'power evangelism' –
that converts were won over by changing their world views
from secular to supernatural. Signs of God's supernatural
power were the proof of his existence and accompanied evangelism – miraculous healing, prophecy, deliverance and the
charismata. Since the mid-1980s claims to supernatural
'signs' were evident in many charismatic churches. When
the Toronto Blessing arrived it was not surprising that it
was largely transmitted through Wimber's Vineyard church

networks. Power evangelism, however, does not always win converts, even if it keeps the converted happy. Rather, it disconcerts and alarms outsiders, draws publicity for all the wrong reasons, and is not conducive to creating the 'safe' environment in which to discover and explore Christianity. *Alpha*, on the other hand, does win converts. Post-Toronto Blessing then, *Alpha* marks a return to Bible study, without the signs and wonders – well, almost.

Chapter 3

Alpha – Strategy, Content and a Few Controversies

Alpha at Holy Trinity

A notice at the entrance of Holy Trinity, Brompton, proudly proclaims the message 'HTB – the Home of *Alpha*'. In a very special way, *Alpha* is HTB's invention.[1] The origins of the course can perhaps be traced back to late 1969 with the publication of the book *Questions of Life* which was conceived as a four-week introduction into basic Christianity at HTB. However, *Alpha* commenced in earnest in 1981 when Charles Marnham, a clergyman at the church, began looking for a means of presenting the basic principles of the Christian faith in a relaxed and informal setting. To start with, *Alpha* was aimed at new converts and was only later extended to non-church-goers when it was noticed that people were bringing along their unconverted friends and associates.

By the time Nicky Gumbel took over, in 1990, *Alpha* was a central feature of the church's life, with the number of participants regularly totalling around 100 people on each course. *Alpha* was then significantly developed by Gumbel in 1992 and has evolved ever since. Under his tutelage the course has become extended in length and more informal in its working philosophy. HTB has continued to refine *Alpha* by sending questionnaires to those who have completed the course. The general idea has been to find out what matters related to the Christian faith truly interest people. In addition, Gumbel also added an important element to the programme – the near-compulsory and controversial weekend away, with its emphasis on the teachings of the Holy Spirit.

Gumbel is the key figure as far as *Alpha* is concerned. As an ex-barrister and Old Etonian, he is very much of the HTB ilk. Giving up a lucrative career in order to become an Anglican clergyman, he has grown into his leading role with *Alpha*. Gumbel has been described to me in various ways. For instance, one clergyman I spoke to pictured him as 'Mr Teflon'. In short, nothing sticks to him. He is squeaky clean – no controversy or gossip surrounds this impeccable figure. However, a number of stories are associated with Gumbel and his link with *Alpha*. These have built up to become almost a mythology. To the fore is one which relates that he was, to use charismatic jargon, 'empowered' by the 'anointing' of John Wimber in the mid-1990s to take *Alpha* nationally. Gumbel's mission, then, is a special one, legitimated by perhaps the most influential evangelist in recent times. It is also this kind of anecdote which more than suggests the continuity of *Alpha* with the broader developments in the charismatic movement over the years.

Today, *Alpha* at HTB is very impressive in terms of its scale and who attends. The church itself claims that most of those who sign up are not committed to the faith but are earnest seekers wishing to know more about Christianity. It may well be, however, that HTB is rather atypical – possibly because it has been running *Alpha* for far longer than other churches and has thus had sufficient time to perfect its strategy and establish wide networks of individuals who constitute *Alpha* fodder. At HTB today there are almost 1000 people attending two courses. On Wednesday evenings some 900 people are involved (of which 200 are leaders and helpers). The same basic strategy is employed. A standard talk on a subject related to basic Christianity is given in the main part of the church – often by Gumbel himself. This large assembly is then broken up into groups of, ideally, 12 people sitting around in a circle to discuss what has been put across. For those who cannot attend the evening course, an alternative is run one morning every week (about 50–100 people attend). In addition, HTB also has 5–6 church 'plants' within a few miles' radius, often in once declining parish churches. Each one has adopted an *Alpha* course and, indeed, most of these 'plants' were established or have grown by running the *Alpha* programme.

Alpha: an evangelical McDonaldization?

At first glance it would appear that a fairly standardised *Alpha* package has been deliberately and systematically exported across the world by HTB. Perhaps, then, it is not too unreasonable to describe it as a form of 'evangelical McDonaldization'. The concept of McDonaldization was developed by the sociologist George Ritzer (1996) who explored the implications of a shrinking global market. Large-scale commerce and manufacturing, dominated by the industrialised developed countries of the West and Japan, now penetrate practically every region of the world in a globalised economy. What is produced is a fairly standard package. Much is typified by McDonald's, the American fast-food chain, which has practically cornered the market in burgers and French fries across the world. Moreover, the McDonald's burger you may purchase in London is very likely to be the same as that you buy in New York, Tokyo, Moscow and anywhere else. It follows that the market dominance of McDonald's, as the 'supply-side' of the burger enterprise, dispels the myth that a 'free' global economy brings endless variation and upholds consumer choice through competition. It is the same all over the world – the same image and the same product. The people want what the people get. In *The McDonaldization of Society*, Ritzer describes how the principles which lie behind McDonald's are spreading throughout the world and into every area of life:

McDonaldization affects not only the restaurant business, but also education, work, health care, travel, leisure, dieting, politics, the family, and virtually every other aspect of society. McDonaldization has shown every sign of being an inexorable process by sweeping through seemingly impervious institutions and parts of the world.[2]

Is it the same with *Alpha*? Has it become a form of evangelical McDonald's? There is much to suggest that it has. Certainly, there is a kind of ideal model of *Alpha* both in terms of its course content and strategy and, given the scale of *Alpha*, the implications are considerable. This is not least of all in terms of how the message is put across, the image of Christianity portrayed, and the theological content advanced. Certainly, the overall strategy of the *Alpha* course, as packaged by HTB, is one which recommends (although by no means insists) that each course should ideally be comprised of twelve people: two course leaders, two helpers and eight guests – a ratio of 3:1 seekers and believers. There is also meant to be a hierarchy of responsibility and accountability: the *Alpha* course team are responsible to pastors, who, in turn (if possible), are accountable to a 'Super Pastor'. To what degree this line of accountability holds, however, and to what extent courses are monitored by those at the top at local level, is far from clear. It is evident, however, that HTB does keep a close eye on how *Alpha* is applied 'on the ground'.

Course content

The content of the *Alpha* programme also belies its tendency towards McDonaldization. Fifteen basic topics have been selected by HTB to be taught over a period of ten consecutive weeks on the standard *Alpha* course. This framework is expected to be rigidly adhered to. These topics present themselves in the form of questions and are as follows:

1. Christianity: boring, untrue and irrelevant?
2. Who is Jesus?
3. Why did Jesus die?
4. How can I be sure of my faith?
5. Why and how should I read the Bible?
6. Why and how do I pray?
7. How does God guide us?
8. Who is the Holy Spirit?
9. What does the Holy Spirit do?
10. How can I be filled with the Spirit?
11. How can I resist evil?
12. Why and how should we tell others?
13. Does God heal today?
14. What about the church?
15. How can I make the most of the rest of my life?

The key questions which automatically come to mind are: what has led to these particular topics being advanced as representing 'basic Christianity'? Who decides what is included under the rubric of each theme and what is left out? Who is the final arbiter? The answers are not straightforward. First, to some extent the content is orientated to answering certain fundamental questions. As we have seen, HTB has conducted research over a number of years to find out what issues are important to non-believers. Hence, we might assume that some topics on the courses will take into account popular demand. Secondly, given its ecumenical and all-embracing nature, *Alpha* is meant to be as broad and inclusive as possible. It is not denomination specific and is intended to be user-friendly to all Christian traditions, calculated not to offend Roman Catholics or Protestants of different persuasions. Neither does it mention contentious issues which have long plagued Christendom, such as infant baptism, the nature of communion or the ordination of women clergy.

A brief glance at the content suggests that the agenda is

firmly set in terms of what is encompassed by *Alpha* and leaves little room for manoeuvre by those who administer it at a local level. There are obviously implications here. It may seem that some topics included in the programme, such as 'Who is Jesus?' or 'Why did Jesus die?', would be vital to any programme on basic Christianity. Areas such as 'Why and how should I read the Bible' probably remain relatively unproblematic (although I suspect that some theological critics would have problems with the interpretation of these themes). However, a number of topics included are perhaps less easy to justify. The three themes on the Holy Spirit, especially 'How can I be filled with the Spirit?', as well as the issue 'Does God heal today?' have run into controversy. Largely this is because they represent the core charismatic component. Why these topics are included was a matter I discussed with Ben Pollard at HTB. I asked him why there was an emphasis upon the spiritual gifts and healing when by no means all Christians would accept that they are an integral part of Christianity today and that to believe so is, for some, theologically unsound. His response was that healing remains relevant to the Great Commission (along with spreading the gospel and casting out demons) and that 'we assume that the emphasis on the charismata is biblical'.

If, in some topic areas, *Alpha* appears to be fairly selective and subjective in what it includes, there is also the matter of what it leaves out. It is reasonable to argue that no very basic course in Christianity can include everything. However, certain themes are conspicuously missing. The more liberal-minded Christian might argue that considering aspects of a social gospel is imperative. Where are the teachings about feeding the poor and bringing social justice? Where is a discussion of the complexity of Christian ethics – the basis of a just war and similar issues? These themes may be discussed on an *Alpha* course but are not automatically flagged up as essential. There are other theological objections besides, not only from liberals, and these will be considered shortly.

However, what can be concluded here is that what is encompassed or excluded remains contentious, given that
Alpha appears to be a standard package.

Course structure

Before outlining the structure of a typical evening on an
Alpha course, perhaps a little more should be said about its
broad strategy and underlying working philosophy. How to
conduct *Alpha* at the grass-roots level is something that HTB
has given much attention to. It is clear that there is a great
deal of implicit sociology and social psychology involved, and
HTB is keen that everyone gets it right. For that reason there
is plenty of literature and 'plastic' media material generated
to support local churches and to enforce the recommended
way of doing things. There is, for example, the HTB-produced
Alpha Team Training audio tapes, where Nicky Gumbel talks
about group dynamics – how people naturally relate together
in the *Alpha* setting and how, within the context of the
course, relationships should develop naturally. People are
therefore encouraged to talk in company, 'be themselves',
and find new friends. Hence, a principal aim of *Alpha* is
to integrate people into a small group and ultimately, it
is hoped, into church life. In addition, there are aids for
church leaders and course administrators such as the
video *How to Run the Alpha Course: Telling Others*, or the
15-minute promotion pack *Introductory Video*, which
includes material from *Alpha* courses and conferences held
at HTB. These, and such tapes as *Alpha Worship*, which has
a '16-track recording of hymns and songs suitable for use on
Alpha', undoubtedly further enhance the tendency towards
McDonaldization.

The strategy behind delivering the *Alpha* course results
from tried-and-tested methods which have been developed
over a number of years. It is a strategy that epitomises the
softly-softly approach to evangelism. As we have seen, *Alpha*
bills itself as an introductory course and endeavours to teach

basic Christianity to the unchurched and unconverted in what is anticipated to be a 'safe' environment which bridges church and secular culture. In most cases it is not run at a church but in somebody's home (which usually means a great deal of hard work for some lay person). What then happens is fairly stringently mapped out. This is certainly true regarding how *Alpha* 'guests' are engaged on the course. The course leaders are advised not to confront people, especially in the early stages, with what is objectionable about their lifestyles, not to condemn such sin as premarital cohabitation. In time, sensitive issues are discussed as part of an exploratory processing and for that reason 'seekers' are encouraged to read Christian books and tapes. Such seekers, so the theory goes, will become aware of their own moral ineptitude, especially with the help of mature Christians who are encouraged to 'pray for God to convict them' (*Alpha Team Training* audio tape). Neither are people to be put on the spot about making a commitment to the faith and only at a later stage might they be asked if they would like a prayer of conversion.

There are a number of other 'don't dos' for those running *Alpha*. If 'guests' are angry and aggressive, if questioning is hostile, antagonists are not to be confronted by course leaders at a personal level. *Alpha* training tapes optimistically advance the view that over a period of time people will come to see the 'truth', quieten down and ultimately gain the conviction to change or at least modify their views. Another 'do not' is for course leaders to avoid criticising other denominations since *Alpha* tries to win the common ground – to be relevant to all forms of Christianity. Hence, the ecumenical integrity of *Alpha* is sustained.

The meal
At the end of each *Alpha* course a meal, sometimes quite an elaborate one, will be laid on. The prospective *Alpha* candidate should note that the quality of food varies between

churches. The gourmet may like to investigate which churches provide the best meals. In my experience, food at Roman Catholic churches is good; so too is that at Methodist churches, although wine is not served! This quality is not, however, necessarily along denominational lines and much depends on who gets the job of being cook and the enthusiasm involved. Some of the meals can be rather basic, others rather more sophisticated. At some Anglican churches you may have to settle for the age-old favourite of tea and cakes. Others, however, are far more elaborate. A not-untypical three-course menu at a Baptist church included:

> Home-made vegetable soup with roll and butter
> Salmon, sauté potatoes and mixed vegetables, red wine
> Chocolate gateaux
> Coffee/cheese and biscuits

Those who have been on the course and those already in the church are encouraged to invite friends to come along and, presumably, as a result of the national initiative, there will be at least some who have contacted the church as a result of poster advertising or leafleting. These 'guests' it is hoped will, after being suitably wined and dined, become the raw recruits for the next *Alpha* course. At such functions a number of people are generally invited to stand up and give a positive appraisal of their experiences on a previous *Alpha* course. The newly won convert, it goes without saying, is a prized asset.

The new guest at the end-of-course meal may be given a leaflet explaining more about *Alpha*. The one that I came across in a village church in the depths of rural Kent was fairly typical. It stated:

WOULD YOU
> like the opportunity to ask someone those burning questions about Jesus, the Bible, religion?

HAVE YOU
> felt the need to learn more about Jesus?

ARE YOU
> interested in Christianity and would like to know more?

HAVE YOU
> heard about *Alpha* and would like to know more?

ARE YOU
> a long-standing Christian who would like a 'refresher' in the basics?

If the answer to any of these questions is 'YES' or if you have any other reason for coming, DO PLEASE COME.

As the course proper begins there may be a preliminary talk on the first night. People may be asked to introduce themselves. Then the programme unfolds in a standard form that will be followed over the subsequent nine weeks. There is usually a meal or, at the very least, some light refreshment provided for all. Here, *Alpha* tends to give away its cultural pretensions. More often than not the meal comes across as a middle-class dinner party and does not always appear to be a suitable setting for the presentation of the gospel. At one Baptist church I attended, the pre-*Alpha* meal was accompanied with a suitable ambience created by candlelight and waiters in smart suits akin to those in an expensive restaurant. The less cultured found themselves awkwardly searching for the 'correct' cutlery and may have wished that they had opted for the local 'Wimpy'. A glass or two of red wine, while undoubtedly making people more relaxed, could also have the effect of muddling the thoughts, inducing tiredness, or, in the case of one young lady in the church, acting in a rather undignified manner.

Eating is calculated to be a common experience and likely to enhance the conditions in which people will begin to integrate into the *Alpha* group. Clearly, there is much to interest the social anthropologist. While in many societies communal eating is an important aspect of social life and has all kinds of cultural and status connotations, in the contemporary world people are not always familiar with eating in company, not even with family members. For those preferring a television supper without company, the *Alpha* meal can be rather intimidating and what appeared to be a cordial evening can be transformed into something of a negative experience. Nervous looks and tentative conversation across the table is to be expected, at least in the first few weeks. Because of the awkwardness of some mealtimes, some churches that I came across had abandoned the meal for a buffet or dispensed with the food altogether.

The video

After the refreshment and a short introduction by a course leader comes the video presentation. This is Nicky Gumbel's forte since all the videos are based around his talks. Each talk systematically attempts to answer the topical question for that evening. In that sense, the video very much sets the agenda (these are constantly being revised in the light of comments about their content and presentation). Each video lasts for about forty minutes. The talks are clear and articulate and punctuated at just the right junctures by moments of humour such as the following joke that was told by Gumbel:

By the way, have you heard the story of the atheist who fell off a cliff, clutched at a tuft of grass and cried, 'Oh God, if you are really up there, help me'?

'Let go of the tuft of grass,' boomed a voice from above.

The atheist hesitated for a moment then said: 'Is there anyone else up there?'

Gumbel is generally seen standing at a rostrum with his notes and Bible open. He is the epitome of the well-groomed, smart but casually dressed Christian, mature in his faith, polite, articulate and accessible. He is usually viewed standing in front of a very large and colourful flower arrangement, which sometimes dwarfs him. His combination of anecdote, humour, simple theology and polite smile is compelling, while an undoubted sincerity shines through.

Gumbel, although a modest man, is a charismatic figure who has come to have something of a following of his own in recent years. The central part that he has to play in the video has made him a celebrity in some church circles. He is particularly popular among the women – older women above all. A kind of fan club has thus developed among those who see him as handsome and debonair – almost a throwback to a 1950s film star. At one church that ran *Alpha*, so I discovered, a number of ladies ranging from 50 to 80 years old only attended because they wanted to see Gumbel. Each week they would huddle excitedly around the television set to see the main attraction. One of them made a special visit to HTB just to see Gumbel personally. It was, she claimed, one of the best days of her life! Such has been the impact of *Alpha*.

The video shows Gumbel speaking to a large gathering of the faithful at HTB, who are also suitably attired in smart but not conservative clothes (along with the occasional zany but not 'risky' sweat-shirt). There are elegant hair-dos and a fair amount of expensive jewellery. The HTB audience listens intently, laughs accordingly and applauds when necessary. This is the image of *Alpha* HTB-style and it is basically the same image for ten weeks. Each weekly video is watched by the *Alpha* group in conjunction with the relevant section of *The Alpha Manual*, which each guest will be following (with the appropriate biblical quotations). Sometimes the helpers on the course will sit next to the guests, with an open Bible. The latter are encouraged to make notes in the manual as they go along, either for their personal edification or to emphasise points to talk about in the discussion groups which follow.

Discussion

The discussion takes up most of the rest of the evening. The ideal *Alpha* gathering of 12–15 people may be divided into two groups. In my experience the discussion usually lasts for about half an hour. It is expected that it will focus upon the topic considered in the video. Hence, for example, 'Christianity: boring, untrue and irrelevant?' is the theme for discussion in the first week. Guests may be encouraged to open the conversation with questions or comments, or, as Nicky Gumbel proposes on one of his audio teaching tapes, course leaders might like to 'sometimes set the agenda by asking awkward questions themselves'.

Course leaders are also advised to be gently argumentative without being intimidating. They should be unobtrusive and low key, and 'listen to the view of others'. Ideally the distinction between leaders, helpers and guests is blurred in this cordial atmosphere. It is expected that by week six or seven people are probably more committed to the course, more relaxed and more likely to be open to both asking questions and responding to questions posed by course leaders. The evening may finish with a prayer. However, since guests may find this intimidating at first, the possibility might merely be talked about to acclimatise people to the prospect of direct communication with the divine. It may be several weeks before the first prayer is heard in earnest.

After *Alpha*

What happens after an *Alpha* course is not so clear-cut. Those guests who see out its duration have various options. They may wish to convert. They may go away and think about conversion. They may decide that it is not for them and never be heard of again. The latter may or may not be contacted by the church. There is meant to be no pressure to be won over to the faith and any follow-up is likely to be 'light'. Alternatively, the guest may opt to take *Alpha* again or sign up for *Beta* or some other variety of subsequent course.

The *Beta* course (which seems to assume conversion) addresses such issues as helping people grow in their faith, discipline in prayer, how to read the Bible, and how to develop spiritual gifts. There are issues of worship, Christian living, the influence of society and the evils of the world, and how to manage your money (for some inexplicable reason). In similar vein is the nine-week course *A Life Worth Living* (based on the Book of Philippians), which utilises a number of 'follow-up' materials to the initial course. Some less convinced about Christianity may wish, post-*Alpha*, to enrol on a *Searching Issues* course, which seeks to develop some of the difficult questions that have arisen from *Alpha*, including: 'Why does God allow suffering?', 'What is the Christian attitude towards homosexuality?'. *Searching Issues* (based, according to HTB, on the seven most common objections to the Christian faith) is also available in book form, as is *Challenging Lifestyles* (19 studies based on the Sermon on the Mount) – dealing with such issues as 'How to have an influence on society' and 'How to handle money' (again!). There is also Michael Green's *After Alpha* (Kingsway, 1998) and similar publications. The opportunities are thus endless once you have completed an *Alpha* course, while the numerous post-*Alpha* videos and books which have been produced add to the ever expanding *Alpha* industry.

Alpha and its critics

To some neutral observers *Alpha* may seem relatively straightforward and unobjectionable. However, by no means all churches have adopted it. In a straw poll which I conducted of a few churches in the Berkshire area there appeared to be several reasons for not doing so (though they knew of it and even considered it). A number of clergy explained that there was simply no time among other church activities to run the course, nor even the time to look into its alleged merits. These explanations, however, frequently masked more fundamental objections. For instance, among the Anglicans who had given it a wide berth were several who regarded themselves as Anglo-Catholic with no tradition of evangelising. 'Not really that type of congregation' or 'would not fulfil the needs of our church' were other responses provided by Anglican clerics who were more traditional in their churchmanship. Another reason given by some clergymen, of different denominations, was that the instigation of *Alpha* would be divisive. In fact, that is the experience of some, since the introduction of the course caused rifts in not a few churches. An elder in a United Reformed Church told me that over half his fellow elders were on the verge of resigning in protest at the adoption of *Alpha*, and claimed that in several URC churches some actually had resigned.

It is clear, then, that not all Christians are impressed by either the content or the methods of *Alpha*. Indeed, one of the most intriguing aspects of the course is the debate that has been generated as to its merits. There are a number of criticisms of its strategy. A fairly frequent response that I received from a few clergymen was the belief that it pressurises people. In other words, it is not softly-softly enough and, more sinisterly, manipulates people through ten weeks of systematic indoctrination. *Alpha*, therefore, becomes cult-like. Hence, there is a fairly captive audience that is subject to the 'feel-good factor' of food and attention, the charismatic leader who instructs an unquestionable message, and the pressure to conform and accept an unconditional set of beliefs.

Others have been more concerned with questioning the logic of the programme. As one critic has put it, *Alpha* starts with the assumption that conversion has taken place in week one and moves in three weeks from 'nowhere to Christian belief and living the Christian life'.[3] After ten weeks, then, the fully fledged Christian is supposed to emerge, ready for what the world has to throw at him or her. In other words, *Alpha* does not do what it claims to do in providing an introduction to the faith and by way of offering a forum for exploration.

Another criticism of the strategy of *Alpha* has been put forward by Martyn Percy's aptly named article 'Join-the-Dots Christianity. Assessing Alpha'.[4] Percy argues that there is very little attempt to present the church as the body of Christ which is the initial repository for the gospel. While there is a discussion of basic doctrine, there is little mention of the historical Church and all its rich and varied traditions. Like many other evangelising initiatives, the assumption is that people are converted first and then think about joining a church. However, this disassociation is problematic. Many converts won over by evangelising missions often fail to be properly inculcated into the Church and it is the Church which gives moral and practical support and builds up faith. While *Alpha* may focus on a local church, there is little appreciation of tradition, the plurality of the Church, or the congregation as a collective with the same beliefs and orientation. The course could thus be improved by a greater concern with the Church and the sacraments, and by ensuring that the material used was more firmly rooted as 'an arm from within the church, rather than an external agent being used as a go-between'.

Theological objections to *Alpha* also abound, and not only because of its charismatic element. While it seeks to teach a broad introduction to the faith, it is evident that one man's 'basic Christianity' is another's heresy. The principal opponents to *Alpha* are, perhaps not very surprisingly, from the more traditional wings of Protestantism and Roman Catholicism. *Alpha* amounts, in many respects, to an ecumenical initiative in which compromise is a key consideration. However, conservative Protestants and Catholics tend to lament each other's involvement. There are also fairly widespread criticisms from those of a more liberal, theologically speaking, disposition. Collectively, these concerns are, in turn, indicative of the state of contemporary Christianity. There may be less fragmentation in the broad Christian Church than there has been for a century or two, nevertheless the attempt to be contemporary and relevant on the one hand, and still cling to the fundamentals of the faith (as perceived by *Alpha*) on the other, means that it is open to attacks from both liberals and conservatives.

Quite predictably, traditional Protestants, particularly of the conservative evangelical variety (many preferring the Fellowship of Independent Evangelical churches to the more charismatically inclined Evangelical Alliance as their umbrella organisation), have taken the theological high ground and used *Alpha* as an opportunity to bash some of their favourite foes, namely charismatics and Roman Catholics. As it was put to me by one pastor I interviewed:

> We find it [*Alpha*] over-manipulative, man-centred, minimalising the sin question and over-emphasising the charismatic element, especially with the notorious Holy Spirit weekend. The fact that Roman Catholic churches can use it without any qualms demonstrates its dismal lack of doctrinal content.

For this conservative Protestant constituency, *Alpha* is another sign of apostasy and a vindication of a rather pessimistic pre-millenarian world-view. Hence, the perceived errors of the 'nominal' Christian churches confirm its own rather élitist and exclusive stance. This is evident in one story related by an Anglican minister I spoke to who had put on *Alpha* in his church. He had distributed leaflets in his parish advertising the course. Later the same evening members of the local Brethren assembly delivered their own leaflets warning of the perils of *Alpha*, specifying where it had doctrinally erred and the dangers of charismatic-style Christianity. The assembly also wrote to the clergyman, demanding that the course be removed, referring to it as 'satanic'.

An interesting theological debate has emerged on several websites and this has allowed some conservative Protestants to vent their fury over *Alpha*. One evangelical outreach which calls itself the Cross and Word Ministries has produced a website communiqué headed *The Alpha Course. Is it Bible-based or Hell's Teachings?* The focus is upon what is regarded as the link with the Toronto Blessing, or as it is stated, '*Alpha* is being used to get people to accept the teachings and phenomena associated with the Toronto Blessing'. On the website too, I came across perhaps the most damning condemnation of *Alpha* by the pastor of an east coast Presbyterian church. *Alpha*, according to this irate clergyman, was 'the course from the belly of the pit of hell'!

The charismatic element, especially teachings on the Holy Spirit, are frequently criticised by the conservative evangelicals. One pastor of an evangelical church I had communication with had considerable theological reservation about *Alpha*. In a rather sophisticated sociological, as much as theological, argument, he insisted that those who had designed the content had little understanding of the nature of God, Jesus or the atonement, or the nature of the Holy Spirit. It was, he claimed, a course for the post-modern consumer society where practically any form of morality was acceptable – where there was no emphasis on sin and guilt. This, he maintained, was reflected in *Alpha*. Moreover, *Alpha*, he insisted, 'presents "a give me now theology" of "I have been through the course, believe – so give me my

reward" '. He concluded that it was well-intentioned but badly
aimed and that: 'People are probably not really converted and
don't change their life-style. Like much of the charismatic
movement, it is based on a lot on emotions.'

A similar kind of reasoning aimed at the charismatic
element is advanced by Chris Hand in his publication 'Is
Alpha Leading People Astray?'[5] 'Leading astray' amounts to
teaching a distorted kind of Christianity that gives too many
concessions to the contemporary world. He suggests in no
uncertain terms that: 'The God of *Alpha* is not the God of the
Bible, the plight of man in *Alpha* is not as serious as in
the Bible, and the Jesus Christ of *Alpha* is not the Jesus
Christ of the Bible.' This type of comment is certainly
congruent with the observations of James Hunter, a long-
standing observer of contemporary evangelicalism. According
to Hunter, Protestant evangelical Christianity, even in very
conservative forms, is increasingly in line with contemporary
culture. Traditional doctrine, particularly that of sin, is
continually under assault. There is the increasing tendency
not to convict or to make people feel uncomfortable. This
is accompanied by a growing preoccupation with self and
self-fulfilment – a concern with feeling and emotion to the
detriment of the traditional doctrine of repentance. For
Hunter, this is the only way that evangelical Christianity
can survive in the modern world outside of sectarian
enclaves.[6]

In some quarters of the Roman Catholic Church in Britain
there is equal concern, but, in many respects, for very different reasons. A handful of bishops are believed to be quite
seriously apprehensive about the use of *Alpha* in some of
their parish churches. Even the Pope is known to have misgivings because of its origins within Protestantism. About
400 Roman Catholic parishes in Britain are running *Alpha*
programmes. I frequently got the impression, however, that
in many instances it was an unsupported fringe programme
and was given the nod by some priests only because it could

reverse Catholic Church membership decline and provided the opportunity to address traditional Catholic moral concerns, such as sex before marriage and the virtues of family life. My broad feeling was that there was a general foreboding about *Alpha* among at least some Roman Catholics. A lively debate can often be followed in parish or diocese newspapers. One reader's letter put things in perspective when it explained that: 'The Roman Catholic Church has its own tradition, it still sees itself as a purer form of Christianity. Hence, *Alpha* is a bit of an anathema to some in our local church.' Moreover, he went on to explain that there still remain considerable doctrinal differences with Protestantism, such as that regarding the nature of Holy Communion, and that many Catholics feared a compromise of their faith. In the course of my study, which included a Roman Catholic church in Berkshire, one of the leaders who run *Alpha* was concerned that the Head of Religious Formation (responsible for Roman Catholic teaching) in their diocese had grave reservations because it was not sufficiently Roman Catholic in its theological composition.

A totally different set of objections are put forward by some liberal Christians, of different denominations, who feel uneasy about *Alpha*. The general contention appears to be that it is too simplistic and that it is promoted in such a way that it is expected to solve instantly all human problems and predicaments. Others fear that the *Alpha* movement is using its financial power to win more influence by ensuring converts are introduced to Christianity through its fundamentalist, specifically Protestant, charismatic and evangelical path. This was the fear of one Roman Catholic priest I interviewed and he cited it as the main reason why he had not run it at his parish church.

This brings us back again to the precise content of the course. Martyn Percy, from a liberal perspective, objects to *Alpha's* relentless appeal to 'basics' – a petition usually associated with a crude form of fundamentalism. The emphasis on 'basics', however, obscures the implicit and explicit paradoxes in the gospel, as well as its breadth. Christianity is offered as an over-simplified, uncontextual project that is 'learned' through a course offering certain types of (charismatic) knowledge and experience. *Alpha* does not self-consciously ask who chose the basics and why they are defined as such. In *Alpha*, the basics reveal themselves as the appeal to a largely inerrant Bible, a powerful Holy Spirit, and the expression of an evangelical atonement theory. They are not, interestingly, the Trinity, baptism, communion or community which might be more appropriate for the needs of some Christian traditions.[7]

Percy's critique also focuses on the over-emphasis on the Holy Spirit. This, he deduces, is because *Alpha* is a product of time and place, and in his words, 'The Spirit on offer obviously arises from a personable, therapeutic, home-counties context that is concerned with the individual.' According to Percy, this focus upon the individual as the receptacle of the Holy Spirit is at the expense of his work in creation, justice, peace and reconciliation. This is because those who put the course together reflect an élite, upper-middle-class outlook which is also applied to the gospel. *Alpha* may attempt to be relevant to modern man but, as clearly seen in its theology of the Holy Spirit, it is anchored in a particular cultural context and Christian milieu.

Another complaint from liberals is that since the *Alpha* course uncompromisingly opposes homosexuality and abortion and promotes celibacy outside marriage, it fails to deal with what are sometimes very sensitive issues. Mary Robins, an assistant priest at St James's in Piccadilly (well known for its active campaigns against fundamentalism) admits that her church helped people who had been damaged by *Alpha*. '*Alpha* [courses] are very black-and-white,' she has claimed. 'I find them very rigid in their view of what it is like to be a woman.' In respect of the money spent on the national initiative, she went on to comment that: 'if my church had

£1 million to spend we would use it to set up day centres and support the Jubilee 2000 campaign to get rid of Third World Debt'.[8] *Alpha*, then, to put it in the form of an understatement, is not to everyone's taste.

Chapter 4

Who Adopts *Alpha* and Why?

The survey

Although *Alpha* has solicited a fair amount of concern in Christian circles, there is little doubting that it has its attractions. The reasons why it has enjoyed such widespread appeal is the subject of this chapter. Hence, we can enquire what kind of churches are prepared to adopt the *Alpha* course and what their reasons are for doing so. These questions are answered by exploring the patterns of adoption, the importance of the charismatic element, and the perceived advantages (as well as some of the disadvantages) of *Alpha* by church leaders and church organisers. Here then, we are concerned with, to use an economic metaphor, the significance of the 'supply-side' of *Alpha*. The 'consumer' side, that is, the motivations and experiences of those who enrol on *Alpha*, will be the subject of subsequent chapters. To begin with, however, a little more needs to be said about the survey upon which this and the following chapters are based – in particular, the sample of churches involved and the broad strategies undertaken in the research.

The survey was based on a number of churches in the county of Berkshire. I contacted (not always with a response) the 129 churches registered in the Reading area phone book in 1999. Forty churches were found to be running *Alpha* courses. To this was added a somewhat higher proportion of churches in Maidenhead, to the east of the county, where nine of the thirteen churches listed in the phone book had adopted *Alpha*. The clergy or *Alpha* course leaders in these churches were approached and asked if they would like to be involved in what amounted to a pilot study. Some agreed to do so.

Of course, a pertinent question is whether Berkshire is typical of other regions of Britain in terms of its economic and demographic structure. In many respects it is probably not. The outlying rural/suburban areas of the county include some of the most affluent in the country. Within Berkshire, however, there are considerable demographic variations. There are rural and urban divides and a number of fairly deprived areas in its major towns. For many years Reading was used in surveys of different kinds because it was regarded as a 'typical English town' by way of its demographic and economic profile. It is now rather less typical but does offer a fairly useful sample of the general population: it has a well-established segment of the population, alongside a sizeable constituency of 'outsiders' from the professional classes, and quite a large Asian community. As far as Maidenhead is concerned, we may note that it has been designated, head for head, the most affluent town in Britain.[1] However, it also has rather less salubrious urban neighbourhoods, council estates, and outlying semi-rural areas which provide a useful contrast. To conclude, while the research is based only on two towns in Berkshire, I believe that generally speaking, the findings reported here are fairly typical of other regions in Britain.

As part of the pilot study, I initially interviewed twenty clergymen or leaders of *Alpha* courses in the Reading and Maidenhead area and administered a small number of questionnaires in their churches. Eight Anglican, three Roman Catholic, two Methodist, five Baptist, one United Reformed Church and one New Church were the subject of the pilot study. These churches had been running courses for various lengths of time, with six joining only in 1998 as a response to the launch of the national initiative.

Number of churches running courses	
Since 1993	4
Since 1996	4
Since 1997	6
1998 (national initiative)	6

Four churches from Reading and Maidenhead volunteered for further, more in-depth research. This included an Anglican church (which I shall call St Peter's) from a more rural area of Reading, and a second church (that I shall call 'Free Church #1') from a rather poor urban locality. A Roman Catholic church (the third largest in the Portsmouth diocese) was selected (I shall refer to it as St Agnes) in Maidenhead – one from a rather less affluent suburban residential area with quite a high concentration of ethnic minorities. I also selected the fourth church ('Free Church #2') from Maidenhead, in this case one which was sited more towards the centre of town.

A total of 400 questionnaires were administered to the four churches (26 per cent of the total to St Peter's, 16 per cent to St Agnes, with the remainder almost exactly divided between the two free denominational churches). The questionnaires were distributed by hand to those who had, over the previous two years, completed the *Alpha* course. The response rate (with questionnaires returned by post) was just over 76 per cent. Some of the questionnaire questions were 'closed', in that they asked for specific details, while others allowed respondents to elaborate upon their views. Administering questionnaires was not always easy since *Alpha* organisers at local churches frequently send out their own questionnaires and, to some extent, there was a duplication of effort. Indeed, on one occasion a church member complained to me that she spent more time filling in questionnaires than attending *Alpha* evenings.

In addition to the administering of questionnaires, forty interviews were conducted of those who had taken *Alpha* in the four churches. The interviews were semi-structured in that I intended to cover specific topics but, at the same time, wished to allow people to freely express their views and recount their experiences. I also spent many hours conducting field work and had myself been through three *Alpha* courses (although not always attending all evenings). To some extent, then, this book relates my experiences as well as those of church leaders administering courses, church members who have helped, and those 'guests' who have enlisted on them.

The pattern of adoption

Let us look, then, at the 'supply-side' of *Alpha* and explore why a fairly sizeable number of churches have opted to endorse it. In short, what is 'the view from the top' regarding its principal attractions and how does *Alpha* come to be adopted in the first place?

In most cases it is the clergy, or other church leaders, who will take the initiative in establishing *Alpha*, although there will frequently be a consultation with church members. It is not unusual for leaders, according to my sample, to send a deputation to another church to find out what *Alpha* is all about. Members of such expeditionary forces may even go through the course themselves. Alternatively, in a few cases, it is the laity who take the initiative and go along to do the exploration. The course is then generally adopted. In the more hierarchically structured Roman Catholic churches, the attitude of the parish priest towards *Alpha* appears to be the decisive factor in determining whether a course will run, although parish traditions and the attitude of parishioners remain important variables and the drive to run a course may initially begin with them.

While three or four of the twenty church leaders interviewed had first heard about *Alpha* either in the Christian or secular media, most had come into contact with it through church networks or had brought the course with them from their previous church. This was especially true of those of a clear charismatic persuasion. Furthermore, five clergy had personal contacts with HTB and a few others had invited HTB representatives to their church to explain what *Alpha* was all about. At St Agnes a course convener explained:

> A friend of mine, a newly ordained priest, had been along to HTB and was impressed by what he saw. He came to see *Alpha* as a way of expanding churches through offering the basics in Christianity and to revitalise the faith. Influenced by him, I bought the video and looked more into the course. Then I went to an *Alpha* conference organised by HTB.

Usually there is a trial run of *Alpha* involving a few church members. Then, once embraced, *Alpha* proper will commence. The means of attempting to enrol people is either through church networks or advertising. The number of courses run, and how often, will depend upon the size of the church as well as the demand. Sometimes, and this was the case in the Free Churches surveyed, *all* church members were asked to go through the *Alpha* course before it 'went public'. This was not always an easy process. In Free Church #2, the first time *Alpha* was run, some 70 people joined, although half a dozen left, complaining bitterly about its content. It was the beginning of a short period of dissent in the congregation.

I also found that one Anglican church appeared to see *Alpha* more as a course in basic Christianity for church members than an out-and-out evangelising campaign, although it was envisaged that this was the long-term aim.

Similarly, St Agnes kept its course, which had run for some three years, exclusively to its parishioners, and was unsure how to take it to non-church members. Posters were tentatively placed on the church noticeboard, rather than publicly displayed. Indeed, course leaders felt that they did not have sufficient confidence or expertise to apply it for public consumption (being particularly self-conscious of their Roman Catholic traditions), although inquisitive members of the public (including sociologists!) were not turned away.

The charismatic element

It almost goes without saying that *Alpha*'s rather charismatic slant appeals to those already of a charismatic orientation. There are, in total, some 24,200 churches in Britain from the various denominations. This means that about one in six have taken *Alpha* under their wing. It might be drawing too much of a conclusion, but approximately 4000 churches were initially involved in *Alpha* at the time of the national initiative. Does this constituency represent a kind of charismatic nucleus? Certainly, it is interesting to note that this is exactly the number of churches said to be involved in the Toronto Blessing at its height in the mid-1990s[2] and by far the great bulk of these were, or became, of charismatic persuasion. If it is true that these churches are charismatic in orientation, they have, over the period in which the national initiative has been launched, been joined by over 2000 others who have been persuaded of the advantages of *Alpha*.

In enquiring about their charismatic allegiances, five of the twenty clergy or *Alpha* leaders I interviewed unashamedly described themselves as 'out-and-out charismatics' or something very much like it. An Anglican curate, responsible for the course in his church, was prepared to identify a strong John Wimber influence running throughout the *Alpha* course. This, he believed, was to be welcomed. His church had previously been of a conservative evangelical tradition but had moved towards the charismatic wing, with many members sympathetic to the charismatic cause. Differences within the congregation had been overcome. The morning service had retained its more traditional element with over two-thirds of the congregation attending. In the evening, the service was for those who preferred a more charismatic way of doing things.[3]

Five church leaders whom I interviewed had an active charismatic element at their church, while a further three estimated that charismatics make up a large proportion of their congregation. In Free Church #1 about 150 of the 400 members were estimated to be of this persuasion. The young, rather traditionalist minister, had some reservations about the course but placated his charismatically inclined members by allowing the *Alpha* course to run. The leader of the course in this church stated:

> I did the *Alpha* training course along with others in the church. I proposed it but there was some resistance because it was too charismatic . . . I would like to see it adopted by all Christian churches. I am a self-confessed evangelical charismatic. The Holy Spirit is important, as charismatics stress, and a relevant theology is needed. I am quite happy to see it open to Roman Catholics and believe that you should worship where you feel comfortable.

Another Anglican minister of an Anglo-Catholic church admitted to me that he was pressurised by the charismatic contingent in his church to take *Alpha* on board and would probably not otherwise have run it. He was by no means the only clergyman I interviewed who felt obliged to do so as a result of grass-roots activity. In most cases these clergy were unhappy about its charismatic element and the possible implications for churches in terms of long-term change and the danger of bringing divisions in the congregation between traditionalists and those who preferred all things contemporary.

While, as I discovered, even one or two clergy who more willingly adopted *Alpha* complained that it was too charismatic, it was sometimes the clergy who led something of an *Alpha* revolution precisely because of its charismatic orientation. One vicar unashamedly explained that he wanted to take his small congregation more in a charismatic direction and that involvement in *Alpha* enhanced this enterprise. This was also the motivation of a Baptist minister of a small congregation who expressed his frustration with '30 years of legalistic conservative evangelicalism which failed to deliver the goods' – that is, to win converts. Moreover, while not themselves charismatically inclined, a number of those interviewed were not opposed to the cause and saw it as a general step in the right direction. The woman who led an *Alpha* course at a Roman Catholic church explained:

> I have always been a Roman Catholic but I am liberal
> in my attitudes. Sometimes being a Roman Catholic is
> frustrating. I have thought about leaving and joining
> the large independent charismatic church in town but
> I decided to stay. I have plenty of disagreements with
> the Catholic Church and personally I am 'low' on
> Mary, the saints and all that. Neither am I a charismatic,
> but I'm not afraid of it.

As far as the Roman Catholics are concerned, it was discernible among some I spoke to that *Alpha* was looked upon favourably in regard to increasing the impact of the charismatic movement in their churches. A letter written to me from a Catholic missionary to Eastern Europe (preferring to remain anonymous) stated:

> *Alpha* is making a break-through in very traditional
> and predominantly Catholic countries. And it is
> precisely in those countries where we especially need

Alpha – to get people to read the Bible, and to make a more direct relationship with God rather than praying though Our Lady or even calling to the saints for help. The charismatic movement is the way forward.

Perceived advantages of *Alpha*

The generally charismatic orientation was one of the most frequent explanations put forward for adopting *Alpha*. Nonetheless, there were a number of others which were often cited as significant and provided a barometer of contemporary evangelical thinking. Perhaps the most commonly expressed view of church leaders was that *Alpha* is user-friendly for several reasons. Firstly, it was commended for not being heavily theological and producing just 'the basics'. Hence, it was non-threatening to those who were 'just looking'. Next, it created a constructive environment and worked through social networks and continued to build on relationships. In doing so, it was believed, *Alpha* may give access to a range of individuals not usually met by other evangelising techniques, and provide people with the opportunity to respond to thought-provoking issues without being especially demanding. As it was put by a Baptist minister I interviewed: 'It only needs one evening per week so does not amount to very much commitment. It's non-intimidating, and not instructed by clergy.'

A second perceived advantage was the way that *Alpha* broke down secular culture. In the words of one House Church representative:

We think that there is a spiritual demand out there. The church is now irrelevant for many. There is the difficulty in persuading people that the church is the answer. There is a huge cultural gap. *Alpha* is just one vehicle of communication.

Similarly, an Anglican minister explained to me that:

It meets people where they are. *Alpha* is a friendly, social and unthreatening way to explore God. You can be a non-believer, a half-believer or already red-hot, everything goes.

And, he continued, in a rather sociological vein:

In the secular world standing on the street corner preaching fire and brimstone does not work. Few people have any idea what you are talking about . . . in the post-modern society people have no knowledge of church or the Bible. The church is a square peg in a rounded world – particularly in terms of its language. People have no church background and the church of today is foreign to them with a foreign language. *Alpha* helps overcome some of these problems.

This last point was reiterated by another Anglican minister who declared that 'sin' was a difficult concept to explain to people. Nevertheless, it could be approached in terms of 'getting your life in a mess'. This was, he pointed out, *Alpha*'s way of putting some of the basics of Christianity across. Others saw the post-modern condition as something of an advantage for *Alpha*. The view was that in contemporary Western society people are increasingly open to ideas of the supernatural. In the competition between Christianity and other faiths it was this supernaturalist element which could be stressed, with *Alpha* offering the forum, and the Holy Spirit weekend providing the necessary 'proof'. And, as one interviewee maintained, 'Christianity has many advantages over the X-Files'.

Thirdly, *Alpha* was applauded for breaking down denominational divides. One of the Anglican churches surveyed provided the venue for dozens of pastors from Reading churches – the great bulk subscribed to *Alpha* (although some had reservations). Hence, *Alpha*, it was accounted to me, allows 'the realisation of the Christian community'. In doing so it has strengthened church unity at a local level and at the same time has ensured that the influence of charismatic Christianity continues to spread through networks of clergy and church representatives.

Finally, there was the obvious argument that *Alpha* wins converts. In talking to some twenty church ministers, such an explanation was mentioned above all others in the context of *Alpha*. This is perhaps not too surprising given that there is the vested interest of boasting a thriving congregation and perhaps one can forgive the preoccupation with church growth, in view of the statistical evidence of church attendance decline. In this respect there was a concern expressed by one elder of a United Reformed Church whom I spoke to about the predominance of elderly people in his church and the conspicuous lack of younger generations to replace them. *Alpha* was perceived to be a way of attracting the young. *Youth Alpha*, however, had failed to get off the ground in this particular church.

With reference to winning converts, some interviewees, in true charismatic movement style, had interpreted *Alpha* as a 'genuine move of the Holy Spirit'. After all, the revival that had been witnessed in Third World countries was now on its way to the West. *Alpha*, then, as one minister declared, 'shows what God is doing today'. Alternatively, in a less excitable vein, some perceived *Alpha* as tapping a latent spirituality. It could allow people to explore the possibility that God exists – thus it was part of a personal quest for some. At the very least, *Alpha* was believed to kick-start people on a spiritual journey or, as it was explained to me by the pastor of Free Church #1:

> The aim is to set people on a spiritual road. It is particularly applicable to the post-modern society and provides key morality where beliefs and values are that of the supermarket and a society of choice according to how we feel. Christianity offers certainty in a world of uncertainty.

Alpha, however, has its disadvantages, even for the most enthusiastic of advocates. Some clergy and course leaders interviewed also recognised down-sides. One complaint was that the general culture of *Alpha* was too middle class. An Anglican minister, in a disappointed tone, explained how a woman had left the course after only one week because the group was predominantly middle class and educated, and that she 'felt left out and intimidated'. Another clergyman had problems with the Nicky Gumbel video presentations and was thinking of starting his own course, complaining that: 'He [Gumbel] is Old Etonian. He is middle class talking to middle-class people. Because of this *Alpha* is a bit intellectually demanding for some people.' At St Peter's, Gumbel's upper-middle-class accent was frequently the source of great amusement. There was a fair amount of fun and frivolity in mimicking his accent as the video progressed. On one occasion a rather radical member of the group described HTB scathingly, on the evidence of the video, as 'a middle-class glee club'.

The second stated difficulty among those who run *Alpha* was that it assumes too much prior knowledge. While critics have lamented its lack of theological grounding, those outside the faith (and some inside) often simply do not understand what is being put across. In this respect, so it was occasionally argued, too much could be expected of *Alpha*. An Anglican minister observed that those being introduced to the Bible for the first time are hesitant and that is often why some give up in the first few weeks. He complained that: 'Initially people are confused and find it very difficult to understand since they have no experience of the Bible. The discussion groups look at the biblical references, but it is lost on people. We had someone on the last course who had never even heard of St Paul.'

Beyond these concerns, a number of other disadvantages were less frequently mentioned and included the felt belief that some important issues are not adequately addressed.

Others thought that there is too much emphasis on the charismata, while, by contrast, some maintained that there was not enough on healing or spiritual warfare. A few individuals, both clergy and lay, argued that *Alpha* tends to present a 'quick-fix theology', that it is pastorally weak, not always practical in dealing with *real* human problems such as divorce or unemployment and, according to one interviewee, 'the world is revealed in a 30 minute package . . . *Alpha* is marketed to provide an answer to everything, but it isn't. It is not the be all and end all even for those of us who readily endorse it.'

Chapter 5

Who Joins *Alpha* and Why?

Most of my eighteen-month research of *Alpha* was concerned with studying those who had experienced the course as 'guests'. As part of the pilot survey, a number of informal interviews were conducted with those who had experienced the course from the 'consumer side'. From the findings of these interviews several broad questions immediately presented themselves. Probably the most pertinent was why people enrolled on an *Alpha* course in the first place – what interested them as outsiders exploring the faith, as the 'just-looking'. Were the relevant issues they wished to explore primarily about the Christian faith itself, or were they concerned with broader topics? As we shall see, the answers to at least some of these questions were not the ones that might have been anticipated. This is largely because the reasons why people join *Alpha* are not exactly those that the national course organisers may have expected or hoped for.

A different range of questions can be asked about what kinds of people join *Alpha*. Is there something distinctive about their social background? If so, are there particular types of people that *Alpha* tends to attract? Conversely, are there categories of people that *Alpha* is unlikely to reach – for example, certain age groups, ethnic groups and social classes? Another part of the equation relates to church background. Is it the case that *Alpha* appeals to those who have some knowledge and experience of the faith, or is it attracting those who are enquiring for the first time? All these key questions relate invariably to the ultimate issue of whether *Alpha* is working. Above all, does it do what it claims to do in providing an opportunity to explore Christianity for the 'just-looking'?

Finding out about *Alpha*

One of the questions asked in the questionnaire was simply: 'How did you get to know of *Alpha*?' As the statistics below show, the great majority of people on an *Alpha* course came to know of it through their Church. The first observation, of course, is that these figures hint at the fact that the majority of those signed up were already in the church. The second observation is that these findings suggest that the aim of the national initiative to move away from social networks to direct advertising has largely failed.

How did you get to know of Alpha?[1]	%
Through my church	69
Friends	15
Media	13
Poster	2
Leaflet	1
Miscellaneous	1

Why join?

Those who were administered questionnaires were also asked the direct question: 'Why did you join *Alpha*?' There were a number of smaller categories of responses which, nevertheless, added up to a sizeable proportion of answers that did not directly appear to relate to a clear pursuit of knowledge about the Christian faith. Some 5 per cent attended *Alpha* for no other reason than that they were involved in running the course for their church. Added to this category was around 3 per cent who stated that their primary reason for joining was that they had been advised to do so by their church leaders or had initially taken the course when it was first introduced as a 'dry run' before going public.

Just over 2 per cent of those who had attended *Alpha* were looking for something to join and admitted that they could have signed up for practically anything. As one middle-aged lady put it: 'It's something to be doing mid-week, isn't it?' About the same percentage claimed that they were 'just curious' or 'inquisitive'. This was a class of people typified by one interviewee who put his reason for joining as 'I wanted to find out what all the fuss around *Alpha* was about rather than explore Christianity per se'. A further 2 per cent had joined because they admitted that it presented a manifest opportunity for a good argument or even to be deliberately provocative. Finally, of this rather miscellaneous category, there were a handful of individuals who were pragmatically taking advantage of an *Alpha* course by way of embracing its hospitality or, as it was unashamedly stated by one respondent, 'free food and company!'

Before considering the larger categories of responses it is worth pondering upon a more 'hidden' attraction of *Alpha*, which was not automatically tapped by interviews or questionnaires. This conjecture that people were not always primarily joining for their stated reasons, results from the observation of a number of clergy or church leaders that I talked to. It is also obvious that this more hidden aspect was not exactly in line with the main aims of *Alpha*. In short, the suspicion of some course leaders was that *Alpha* had become something of a pastoral tool for helping people with emotional and psychological problems, rather than a means of evangelism. This was illustrated by one interviewee who explained: 'We had one seventy-year-old man who was on the course.

He had just lost his wife. *Alpha* gave him a focus in his life rather than a spiritual journey.'

An Anglican minister recounted that *Alpha* provided the context in which church leaders could deal with people who were lonely or hurt, or even had deep psychological conditions. In his very middle-class parish, so he alleged, there were quite a few professional people on the course whom he described as 'emotionally disfunctional'. This was, he explained, generally because of some past emotional trauma or more recent personal difficulties related to the state of their marriage or anxieties resulting from insecure job prospects. *Alpha*, he went on to argue, had the effect of binding people into small groups, hence providing a sense of belonging and making individuals feel good about themselves, appreciated and valued. In some cases *Alpha* replaced aspects of home and family life. This particular clergyman admitted that he had basically given up the stated objective of the course and used it primarily to deal with people's personal problems. Since *Alpha* could work in this way, it may explain why some individuals take the course for a second or even third time. The questionnaire survey indicated that 5 per cent of people admitted that they had attended at least two courses. For some, then, *Alpha* can become rather addictive at least partly because it addresses personal problems, besides the more obvious function of simply providing company. It may well be that, nationwide, around one in twenty people are repeating the course for various reasons. These people have become increasingly known in some churches as 'Alphaholics'. While HTB, as I understand it, encourages people to take the course again, it is probably not for the reason hoped for – that is, to have a deeper understanding of the faith.

The second largest category of people attending *Alpha* courses, about 16 per cent, were those who insisted that they primarily did so because they were invited or persuaded by others to attend. Hence, friends, relatives or work associates had brought them along. (Around 1 per cent of total respondents put as their main reason for attending *Alpha* the simple explanation that they were accompanying their spouse.) Many in this category admitted that they felt obliged to attend and had no real interest or commitment. Indeed, a number stated that they would probably have dropped out if they had not felt morally beholden to see it through as a result of loyalty to someone they knew. This constituency appeared to remain fairly sceptical about *Alpha*. There were few new converts won here.

A more willing contingent were those who had commenced an *Alpha* course because they either knew of somebody connected with a church or had, on the fairly rare occasion, responded to the advertising campaign of the national initiative. It is this group of people, along with other categories discussed below, who seemed to have joined for what might be interpreted as a genuine motivation to know more about Christianity. This was a fairly wide representation of people who preferred to say that they joined *Alpha* because they were generally 'interested in finding out more about religion'. This amounted to around 5 per cent of respondents who were outside of the faith, had little previous knowledge of Christianity, and largely appeared to be on an earnest spiritual journey. This was couched in often vague questionnaire responses such as 'searching for something', 'to get answers to questions', 'to fill a spiritual void' and 'curiosity and maybe to prove something' or, as one person put it, 'I had questions concerning the existence of God'. It was certainly my impression that this category was constituted by true 'seekers' – probably the real segment of the population that should ideally be responding to the *Alpha* initiative.

Alpha, it appeared, also established the necessary networks. As one interviewee disclosed: 'I can understand why people would be intimidated by going to church. *Alpha* brought me in.'

The third largest category of people joining *Alpha* (some 14 per cent) were those already convinced of their Christian faith and who were using it as a kind of refresher course. Indeed, 4.4 per cent of questionnaire respondents specifically mentioned that *Alpha* provided them with a 'refresher course' or something very much like it. Typical questionnaire responses included:

- 'I was interested in the content of *Alpha* plus a need to revive the "basics".'
- 'I wanted to go back to Christian fundamentals.'
- 'To reassure my faith.'
- 'To blow away a few cobwebs.'
- 'To re-establish general Christian principles.'

This latter category is probably part of the largest contingent of 'guests' at *Alpha* courses who are already committed Christians. However, I think that they are worth keeping separate since their needs are rather different in that they were, for the most part, seeking a kind of personal spiritual renewal after a period of backsliding, scepticism or dis-illusionment.

What, then, was the largest category? These were people who appeared to wish to deepen their faith, often by increasing their knowledge of the doctrines of Christianity. They were, therefore, already committed Christians, or in some cases, people on the fringes of the church. They con-stituted some 66 per cent of questionnaire respondents. Statements typically given as to why they joined *Alpha* included:

- 'To learn more about Jesus, Christianity and the Bible.'
- 'To seek a greater understanding of Christ.'
- 'I thought it would be good to get more of an insight into the Bible.'
- 'I wanted to broaden my faith.'
- 'To answer questions about my faith.'
- 'Searching to make my Christianity relevant and real.'
- 'Wanting a better understanding of God'.

The individuals who comprised this constituency, then, sought to grow in their faith rather than to rediscover it. Indeed, around 6.5 per cent of these respondents specifically cited the need for personal 'spiritual development' or 'growth'. A few respondents also showed evidence of changing their denominations and churches on several occasions over a period of years precisely for this reason.

The pursuit of spiritual growth was a conviction which came out more clearly during interviews. One or two respondents felt that their church, or previous churches they had belonged to, had not delivered the goods. As one interviewee put it: 'I signed up because I wanted to know God better. People have been let down by their churches. They may go through baptism or confirmation. But often that's it, you have to then fend for yourself. The churches do little in the form of guidance as where to go from there.' Similarly, another interviewee stated: 'I very much wanted to explore the basis of my faith – my own church does not provide much in either opportunity or support in this area.'

The question which is automatically raised is whether British churches are failing in some of their major functions. This is not only in terms of winning converts, but by way of allowing people to grow in their faith. The possibility remains that one of the key reasons that people drop out of the church is because they cannot develop their Christianity. This is a theme which has been explored by other commentators. In *Gone But Not Forgotten*, a book which attempts to grapple with the reasons behind church-leaving, Philip Richter and Leslie Francis regard the felt need of people to mature in their faith as one of the principal reasons for doing so.[2] Richter and Francis recognised the complexity of the issue in that people are at different stages in their faith and may need special requirements. Nonetheless, the message is clear in that their survey indicated that 'Churches were not always able to provide the opportunities for growth that leavers wanted'.[3] *Alpha* may, therefore, merely be showing up some of the inadequacies in this area.

Church background

The distribution of a small number of questionnaires constituted part of the pilot study at an early stage of my research. From these I was able to discern the rather surprising fact that a fairly large majority of people who enrolled on *Alpha* courses were already in the church. It was only later that I became aware of the size of this contingent and that this was mostly for reasons of spiritual development or for a refresher course, or otherwise advised by the church leadership to attend.

Respondents were asked the simple question: 'Have you ever belonged to a previous church?' It was found that the great majority were members of the church who were running the course. In addition, a number of individuals from other churches attended *Alpha* courses because their own church had not set one up. A further 7 per cent were non-churched, the majority of which were non-believers. Finally, there were those who could be described as agnostics but who had some experience of church life in the past. This category ranged considerably in terms of their denominations, from Roman Catholic to Pentecostal. Typical responses in questionnaires from the latter group of people included:

- 'As a child I went to a Baptist church every week but faded away.'
- 'Born a Roman Catholic, and that was it really.'
- 'I was a choirboy when young. That was my only reason for going to church.'
- 'As a child I was sent to a Catholic church.'

Many of this category of people, on the evidence of the questionnaires, appeared to be considering returning to the faith (and church) after a fairly long period of absence. Numerous reasons were presented for having giving up. However, the profile was of a cluster of individuals seeking to explore or reconsider their faith in later life.

Church background	%
Already in the church running course	77
Belonging to other churches	3
On fringes of church running course	4
Agnostics with some experience of church life	9
No church experience, non-believers	7

The general picture which emerges is that, in terms of those who join *Alpha*, there are a number of overlapping circles of interests. These circles are comprised of people according to their commitment to the faith and, probably, their knowledge of it. Those at the core are largely those already dedicated to Christianity but wishing to develop spiritually or to experience a 'refresher course'. In addition, there are a number of prodigal sons (and daughters) returning or considering returning to the faith, probably at a later stage of life. Next are those who are outside of the faith (about 1 in 20) but who are earnestly exploring it as part of a spiritual quest – the real '*Alpha* people'. What *Alpha* brings to all of the above is a distinct form of Christianity that is essentially charismatic in orientation. Beyond these categories of people are a rather miscellaneous group of individuals who have a variety of 'non-religious' reasons for being involved.

Searching issues
As we have seen, *Alpha* seeks to provide an introduction to basic Christianity. An important element of this is the opportunity for 'guests' to discuss issues important to them.

My research allowed the possibility, through questions and interviews, for respondents to state what the significant topics or essential 'searching issues' are. In the question-naires, respondents were asked: 'What issue related to Christianity would you most wish an *Alpha* course to address?'

Searching issues	%
Suffering	50
Other religions	15
Sex before marriage	5
Homosexuality	6
Faith and science	5
Contradictions between the God of the Old Testament and that of the New	5
Other theological questions	10
Miscellaneous	5

As noted earlier, Holy Trinity, Brompton, has conducted research into this precise area. My own conclusions were largely in line with its findings. Top of the bill was the problem of suffering in the world and how this seemed to be irreconcil-able with the character of a loving God. As one interviewee explained:

> I wanted to know about suffering. People on the course gave me answers like God wanted to give us a choice so we can do things wrong. My niece was killed, so this has helped me cope with things.

Then there was the matter of 'other religions', not only the other world faiths, but the New Religious Movement and the New Age. It was not merely problems of the judgement and eternal destiny of earnest believers of these faiths that was at issue, but what they actually believed. What, for example, did Islam and Sikhism stand for and what were the similarities and differences when compared to Christianity? These were questions not always comprehensively answered by *Alpha* course leaders.

Matters related to sexual morals, such as sex before marriage and homosexuality, appeared to be less contentious issues than the findings of HTB suggest, although these controversial topics were more likely to be raised by the young. My view was that this tended to reflect the fact that the great bulk of subscribers to *Alpha* were convinced Christians and had already made their minds up on these issues. At the same time, there were a number of deep theological topics which have always concerned Christians, such as the mystery of the Trinity or the apparent contradictions between the God of the Old and New Testaments, which were frequently raised. Others, often concerning whether personal life events are a result of God's interventions, were not infrequently brought up. Finally, some questions were denomination specific. For instance, with those respondents who were Roman Catholic, issues such as prayer through Mary or the saints were frequently raised.

Social background

We can now turn to the findings which relate to the social background of those who join *Alpha*. The first observation is that, in some respects at least, a number of demographic features are not dissimilar to the findings of *Christian England*, regarding the social background of church attenders and members (probably the most comprehensive study of churches of late).[4] Given that near-on four-fifths of those sampled on *Alpha* courses were already in the church, there is not too much here to surprise us. At the same time there are few significant departures from the findings of *Christian England*.

Social class

There are various ways that social class can be measured. One is occupation, another is education, and there is a close link between the two. *Christian England* has little to say about social class – presumably because of the lack of cred- ible criteria for measuring what social class actually is. It might be expected that many of the churches surveyed were constituted by middle-class people. After all, numerous studies of charismatic churches have indicated a largely middle-class following attracted by an expressive form of Christianity with other allurements such as emotional healing techniques.[5] Moreover, influential sociologists such as Roy Wallis have documented the general appeal of the charismatic movement to the more affluent sections of the population in terms of core middle-class values, including self-realisation and personal achievement translated into themes of spiritual development. Hence, the movement, through its principal beliefs and practices, offers release from the constraints of negative thoughts and behaviour, and creates a safe environment in which believers can cope with the personal problems thrown up by social roles in the family and the work place.[6]

This range of arguments is convincing and sophisticated. Although there is not the scope to explore them fully here, it is noticeable in our sample that the middle class, or more precisely the lower middle class, is over-represented (see table below). Perhaps it would be prudent, however, not to read too much into this. Firstly, there are other important variables to consider, such as age and gender, which cut across the significance of social class. Secondly, the occu- pations which are generally accepted as comprising the middle class are over-represented in the work force and our sample merely reflects that composition. Indeed, the range of occupations which could be described as 'working class' or 'middle class' are fairly representative of the population as a whole.

Those who subscribed to *Alpha* were drawn from right across the occupational spectrum. There were a smattering of upper professionals, including a scientist and a surgeon, as well as highly qualified accountants and higher ranking managers of firms or public bureaucracies. At the other end of the spectrum there were a few manual workers, although most tended to be skilled, such as plumbers and electricians, rather than semi- and unskilled workers. The largest selection of occupations were those who were lower professional, such as teachers, librarians and administrators. To these can be added clerical workers and those working in the service sector. It is these last categories which ensured that the lower middle classes were over-represented in the sample. One important broader point to note here, in terms of social class, is that these middle-class groups may also be self-perpetuating in that *Alpha* largely works through network contacts – proving the principle that like really does attract like.

Occupation	%
Upper professional	5
Lower professional	26
Clerical/Administrative	55
Skilled manual	10
Semi- or unskilled manual	5

This rather middle-class profile of *Alpha*, as judged by occupation, was reinforced by educational profile.

Highest educational qualification	%
Professional qualification	10
Degree	23
Diploma/Certificate	39
A Level	10
GCSE	9
Less or none	9

Before leaving the area of occupation, it is perhaps worth noting that about one-third of those attending *Alpha* courses were not in fact in paid employment. Of these, one half were retired, and a further third housewives. There were no significant differences between those working and those not working in terms of a previous occupational profile, father's occupation, education and rates of social mobility. However, the fairly high rate of those attending who were not in paid employment may mean that *Alpha* is more attractive to those who have more free time and fewer obligations to others (the retired?), as well as those who may be freer to organise their time (housewives?).

In work	%
Employed	65
Not working	33
Not stated	2

If not working	%
Retired	46
Housewife	34
Disabled	11
Student	9

Gender

It is perhaps in the area of gender where *Alpha* better approximates broad church attendance figures. *Christian England* found (or otherwise presents evidence) that a greater percentage of church-goers are female (58 per cent in England, 62 per cent in Wales, and 63 per cent in Scotland). *Alpha* courses were constituted as follows:

	%
Male	34
Female	66

The subject of female over-representation in the churches is not one which has frequently been explored. Among the more sophisticated works is that of Tony Walter, who argues that the higher rate of church-going among females can be attributed to a search for solutions to a number of negative social and psychological experiences.[7] Feelings of guilt, anxiety, emotional difficulties generated by domestic roles, and dependency on the male sex, are frequently concerns which need to be psychologically addressed. Compensators might also be sought for such deprivations as poverty, low status and lack of opportunities, again linked to the limitations of female social roles and child-rearing in particular. These are complex and contentious issues and there is not the room to discuss them here in detail. Although not specifically observable from questionnaires or interviews, it is more than possible that *Alpha* is providing positive functions for women by perhaps fulfilling social and psychological needs and, in the long term, by encouraging integration into church life. Much remains speculative.

Age

Our sample found that there was a fairly wide spread of age categories of those taking *Alpha* – ranging from 20 to 84 years old. Beyond that, we can observe that *Alpha* is popular with a wide range of people between 30 and 70.

Age	%
–20	2
21–30	7
31–40	37
41–50	26
51–60	14
61–70	10
70+	4

In some respects this is surprising as the assumption of many clergy and church leaders was that it was the 30–40 age category that *Alpha* overwhelmingly attracted. While those joining *Alpha* were from a fairly wide spread, the under 30s and over 70s are, however, conspicuously missing. The latter could feasibly be accounted for by physical incapacity or failure to identify with the charismatically orientated *Alpha* course and its contemporary form of presentation. Indeed, several course leaders I interviewed felt that the course did not work well for those at this end of the age spectrum. Then there is the relative absence of those under 30, especially the under 20s. This is not good news if *Alpha* is seeking to win over a new generation of church-goers. With one notable exception, where in one Anglican church *Alpha Youth* invigorated and expanded the youth group, I found in the survey that all other attempts to establish such groups had spectacularly failed. In theory, new young converts could be won over, but the problem is that 'cold evangelism' directed to this age group seems unlikely to work.[8]

The matter of the next generation of church-goers (or lack of them) cannot be underplayed. Peter Brierley, in *Christian England*, points out that socialisation into church life is an important ingredient in sustaining the young in the faith. In recognising the difficulties in doing so, he quotes Reginald Bibby, author of *Fragmented Gods*, a major book on Canadian church life who states:

> As things stand, there will be an ongoing decline in church attendance during the 1990s. The reason is simple: people who attend as adults are primarily people who attend as children. Active churchgoers seldom come out of nowhere; they are homegrown. And the proportion of children being exposed to religious instruction outside the school day has dropped from three in four to less than one in four at present.[9]

Brierley believes that the situation is more or less the same in Britain. Evangelising the young, then, remains one of the major challenges of the contemporary church. For the moment, at least, *Alpha* does not appear to be the vehicle for doing so.

Of the people who might be described as middle-aged, those between 40 and 60, the sample of *Alpha* course guests indicated a higher proportion of individuals who were not in the faith but who might be described as part of that small constituency of 'earnest seekers' or others who were returning to church life after a rather long period of absence. As far as the latter is concerned, there is probably a great deal to concur with Richter and Francis' findings. A large component of church-leavers are those who give up church in their teenage years or early twenties because of other distractions and family responsibilities.[10] *Alpha*, then, may be a way back for those wishing to return to the fold in mid-life, perhaps after their children have left home and they have settled down into secure patterns of work and social life.

Ethnicity

Ethnic groups	%
White	97
Asian	1
Other	1
Not stated	1

There is probably little to say about ethnicity. The sample of churches surveyed were unrepresentative of the population as a whole in that their congregations were white. At the same time, it is my observation (and only mine) that very few black churches (which are usually of the Pentecostal persuasion) have endorsed *Alpha*. There may be various reasons for this. The most obvious is that its general orientation (although undoubtedly not intended) is towards the white middle classes.

Marital status

To complete the picture we can say something briefly about marital status. The high percentage of those married may reflect the age composition of *Alpha* groups, as may the number of widowed, while the relatively low number of divorces probably reflects the Christian moral attitudes of a predominantly church-based constituency.

Status	%
Married	70
Single	14
Widowed	11
Divorced	4

This chapter has largely been concerned with exploring what types of people are attracted to *Alpha* courses and why. Some findings are clearer than others, while further research is obviously necessary in some areas. One thing for sure, nonetheless, is that *Alpha* is not reaching certain sections of the population despite the saturation advertising of the national initiative. In contrast, some people are over-represented both in terms of social background and church experience. In that respect, *Alpha* may not be living up to its principal aims. However, its success can be measured in ways other than who it attracts. This will be the subject of the next chapter.

Chapter 6

Alpha on the Ground: Some Observations

What are people's experiences of *Alpha* at the local level? Given the reasons why people join an *Alpha* course, we might ask whether it fulfils their expectations. Hence, we can explore the alleged benefits (or otherwise) it has to offer. Then there is the key question as to whether it delivers what it is supposed to by way of endearing people to Christianity and winning a significant number of converts. First, however, there is a related issue to consider. The previous chapters of this book have outlined the working philosophy of the *Alpha* course as envisaged by Holy Trinity, Brompton. But how does theory translate into working practice in churches up and down the country? Is the package quite so uniform as might be suggested at first glance or are there considerable adaptations and local variations? In this chapter we will see that sometimes variations do exist and that there may be significant implications here for the *Alpha* initiative.

Variations on a theme

In Chapter 3 we saw the possibility that *Alpha* may be seen as a kind of evangelical McDonaldization – a prepacked course which has rapidly made its way around the world. But is this true in the way that *Alpha* actually operates on the ground? In their discussion of globalisation, sociologists have also come to speak of processes of 'localisation'. Globalisation can mean homogenisation – the standardising of a mass-produced commodity. At the same time, paradoxically, diversity and fragmentation are also features of globalisation and even the most standard package may be transformed almost out of all recognition.[1] In short, there may be some forces which work against McDonaldization at a local level as a result of institutional, economic and cultural influences. It may well be that in manufacturing and commerce a uniform package will be intended but this is not how things necessarily work out (even McDonald burgers are not entirely the same the world over). As far as local adaptations to religion are concerned, there may not be anything particularly new here. Christianity began two thousand years ago as a set of simple doctrines and practices. However, over time, and in different cultural contexts, it has been significantly modified or metamorphosed. So it is with *Alpha*.

In transforming aspects of *Alpha*, the importance of denominational characteristics have a key role. *Alpha* was designed to be friendly to all denominations. In theory it concentrates on the core elements of the faith which are supposedly hard to deviate from. However, it was accepted by many course leaders who were interviewed that *Alpha* is bound to reflect denominational differences. This does not always amount to deliberate attempts to change or even distort the initiative. Occasionally, however, the customisation of *Alpha* appears to come close to it. Tradition and doctrinal preferences are not discarded overnight and to some extent they impinge upon the structure and philosophy of the course. The key question is whether this compromises its integrity. The vicar of a traditional Anglican church admitted to me that under his auspices *Alpha* takes the form of Anglo-Catholicism. This is not only by way of the core themes which *Alpha* addresses. It was also apparent in the two or three weeks of teaching which are tagged on to the end of the course in order to advance the traditions and practices of Anglo-Catholicism. Similarly, a Baptist minister instructed his course leaders to run the programme within the framework of Baptist traditions and to further the cause not only of his denomination, but of Protestantism generally. This was much to the consternation of two Roman Catholic ladies who left the course after only two weeks.

Perhaps the most notable transfigurations which take place on *Alpha* courses are within the context of Roman Catholic churches. One leader at St Agnes put it to me that it was the intention of her church to win people over to Christianity, not Roman Catholicism. However, she and other Roman Catholic church leaders to whom I spoke, were aware of their implicit, if not explicit, bias towards Catholicism. This was often self-consciously counteracted. For instance, when praying at the end of an *Alpha* evening, there was a preference at St Agnes for 'hail Father' rather than 'hail Mary', while mention of Mary, the saints and communion were played down. There was also the discernible playing up the virtues of Protestantism in order to foster an ecumenical spirit. At the same time, nonetheless, it was felt that while a standard *Alpha* course should be taught throughout all the denominations, it might be necessary at the end of the course to talk further about things relevant to Catholicism – this was especially thought to be so for those already in the church.

In Britain, the Catholic Church has produced the booklet *How To Support Alpha for Roman Catholics*. The publication claims not to be a Catholic version of *Alpha*. Rather, it is directed towards answering the kind of questions that Catholics ask about the course and, as it declares, is aimed at 'allaying fears that *Alpha* is not doctrinally sound or is too evangelical'. The Catholic *Alpha* Office (established in 1996) has also produced two videos directed at Roman Catholics within the context of *Alpha*: *Why should I listen to the Church?* and *Why should I go to Mass?*

Adaptability and flexibility were accepted by many of the clergy interviewed as one of the advantages of *Alpha*. These are also recognised as strengths by HTB. However, there are limitations. For HTB, it is important not to exclude important elements. As Ben Pollard from the church put it to me: 'It is flexible on the ground to a certain degree but not beyond the spirit of the course.' By way of illustration we may note that course leaders are instructed not to leave out the section on the Holy Spirit. For such reasons *Alpha* is accompanied by a copyright statement on behalf of HTB. Through the statement, HTB suggests that it has always been keen to permit individuals who are running an *Alpha* course the flexibility to adapt it where it was felt necessary to allow for particular local needs. However, it claims that there have often been misunderstandings and that the 'loss of integrity in some courses has given rise to considerable confusion'.[2] In many respects these fears are well-founded and, despite the copyright status, what calls itself *Alpha* may contravene trading standards!

Clearly, variations in the number of people enrolled on any particular *Alpha* course is not that big an issue. However, the numbers may vary beyond the recommended 12, and in my survey ranged from 5 to 30. This may have implications in terms of group dynamics particularly if they are not broken down into smaller discussion groups. Perhaps of more concern are the deliberate changes in the content of the course made at a local level. I came across one Anglican and one Roman Catholic church that omitted the entire section on the Holy Spirit. A course taught at a Salvation Army citadel ran a more streamlined version. This omitted five topics, including the three on the Holy Spirit, which were replaced by the single topic 'What about the Holy Spirit?'

Another church reduced their course to eight weeks – merging together some of the weekly themes. Frequently some churches diluted teaching of speaking in tongues or healing. Two churches did not use videos (not compulsory), but utilised their own material, which was not that officially accompanying *Alpha* (this customisation seems to be increasing in many churches). One of these, a House Church, brought in its own printed matter which, it was claimed, 'added a more personal touch' by including material and themes not on the course, and even set up what was referred to as 'unofficial *Alpha* courses for friends'. Finally, by way of example, one Anglican church used merely some of the *Alpha* programme and only then as the basis of confirmation classes.

On the ground

On the ground, at the local church level, *Alpha* does not always live up to the glossy image of the slick advertising for the course. There was always the very human element to be observed. It is not that any of the courses I attended turned out to be disastrous – far from it. They were generally well organised and well executed. However, like any other aspect of life, *Alpha* could become rather ritualised and lose its momentum. This is why, as I discovered in some instances, there were often long periods between holding *Alpha* courses.

Those who had run the course for some time not uncommonly admitted to being exhausted, overworked, and rarely helped by others in the church. These are the unsung heroes and heroines of *Alpha*. There were those tidying up draughty church halls late into the evening. There were the women cooking (and it generally was women) for the assembled, week after week. And there were those who opened their homes to strangers – some not entirely of a pleasant disposition. A few leaders, desperately tired after the end of the working day or looking after a family, just about survived. Exhaustion sometimes wore down both course leaders and their guests. The entire course often seemed very long, and sometimes too was an evening with *Alpha*. It was not unusual for people to fall asleep during the video presentation and, to the bewilderment or amusement of those huddled together for discussion, someone might do likewise when a key point concerning the relevance of Christianity or one of its core doctrines was being discussed.

There were also times of disenchantment, alongside

happier moments. One evening an elderly woman admitted to the rather embarrassed gathering that if people were converted by *Alpha*, then they should find another church, complaining that it was not until she enrolled for *Alpha* that anyone spoke to her. She had been attending the church for twenty years. 'If they come here,' she announced in no uncertain terms, 'they really will find out that Christianity is boring, untrue and irrelevant!' I would not, of course, suggest that this sentiment is widespread, but it did provide insights into one particular church.

There were other uneasy occasions. At such times coping strategies came into play. This was most evident during discussion time. An honest disclosure from a course leader said a great deal:

> I think that it must happen regularly that people ask questions in the hope that someone will enlighten them, but they remain none the wiser. This happens with us. It can sometimes be a bit like the blind leading the blind!

In discussions after the video presentation people usually behaved with a certain amount of decorum. Sometimes, since most present were converted to the faith, everybody agreed about everything with an embarrassing uniformity – there was no dissension in the ranks. Occasionally, there were long periods of silence with just the occasional nodding in agreement. But there could be more awkward episodes. The topic 'How should we pray?' was not on the face of things particularly controversial. However, at St Agnes it became a difficult issue. Matters became confusing when some in the group spoke of their habit of praying to Mary or the 'Sacred Heart'. Others claimed they prayed to the saints. A lady, steeped in the charismatic movement, acknowledged the importance of the saints but sternly corrected the assembled by saying that prayer is 'through' the saints or Mary not 'to' them. Some dispute followed. Course leaders attempted to defuse the situation by making light of the subject. One claimed that he prayed to St Anthony when he lost things, sometimes with success. However, an elderly woman who had been asleep most of the evening suddenly woke up, to everyone's surprise, and disagreed with the course leader. She claimed that it was all nonsense and pointed out (in no uncertain manner and with a few expletives) that in her experience she had often prayed to St Anthony when she lost something but that it rarely turned up again! Guests and course leaders were highly embarrassed. It was, in the words of A. A. Milne in *The House at Pooh Corner*, when Eeyore fell in the river and drifted helplessly down stream, 'an anxious moment'.

Experience of course

Let us turn to the guests' experiences of the *Alpha* course. I would say that the impression was largely favourable, although the rather courteous replies of questionnaire respondents were often supplemented by more frank interview responses. The questionnaires administered asked the simple questions: 'Having joined *Alpha*, what were your impressions?' and 'What do you think the advantages of *Alpha* are?'. The responses were as follows:

First impressions	%
Good format	29
Helpful in some way	19
Good discussions	11
Good for evangelism	9
Dislike videos	8
Ecstatic/Hallelujah-type response	7
Simple to understand	3
Generally negative	3
Increased knowledge	2
Miscellaneous	9

Advantages of Alpha	%
Good for spiritual development	18
Good format	18
Discussion	17
Simple to understand	13
Non-threatening	13
Relevant to modern world	10
Good fellowship	10
Increased knowledge	6
'Back to basics'	5
Not stated	4
Miscellaneous	1

In the interviews I often asked the question 'Was *Alpha* what you expected it to be?' There were many positive responses:

- 'It was very alternative without being patronising or pushy. All arguments were presented on logical evidence and not just fanciful claims. It was good to be able to ask questions and learn from other Christians.'
- 'Excellent. Nicky Gumbel was simple to understand.'
- 'Very slick and professional.'
- 'Plenty of food for thought. Not over-simplistic.'
- 'I found it interesting and enjoyable, the mix of Christian teaching and group discussion helped me to deal with a fundamental issue, suffering, which had previously been a major reason for not believing in Jesus.'
- 'Thoroughly enjoyed the course at the time. In particular, I gained from the talks and group discussions.'
- 'Well organised, run in a pressure-free environment, friendly people, good coverage of issues over the course.'
- 'It does work for many people. Although I do not agree with all the presentation of the course. It's amazing how people listen to Nicky Gumbel for so long.'

- 'Really enjoyed it. It gave me more understanding of my faith.'
- 'I enjoyed it. I met people with the same interests but different views to myself.'
- 'It has broadened my view for the better.'
- 'It was very informative and helped me understand a more "modern" stance of Christianity.'

In addition, questionnaire respondents were asked what they thought the main weakness of *Alpha* was. There was a wide variety of answers.

Disadvantages (main objections)	%
Video	30
Structure of course	10
Theological objections	5
Limits to discussion	5

Negative interview responses

Overall criticism of the course

- 'It was a good idea to include a meal, but I was disappointed with the course.'
- 'Poor course.'
- 'Not my view of Christianity.'
- 'It's all rather curious, really.'

Discussion groups

- 'I found it quite hard at the beginning – probably because I am shy rather than because of the actual course itself. However, the discussion groups afterwards felt a bit like a college tutorial to start with.'

- 'The people on the course were not very forthcoming in discussion.'
- 'I found the group discussion times hard.'
- 'Discussions could have been led a bit more imaginatively.'
- 'Some dominated discussion, the leaders did not bring out the point of view of others.'

The video

- 'I found some difficulty in warming to Nicky Gumbel in the videos.'
- 'The video was rather long. We needed other video aids.'
- 'The video tapes, apparently a shortened version, were far too long. I found myself falling asleep after twenty minutes and missing the last half hour.'
- 'I did not react very favourably to the Nicky Gumbel tapes. They were too long and boring.'
- 'The videos were far too long. Most people thought so too. A lot of it was not relevant. I don't think you can ask people to pay attention for such a long time on a hot afternoon. You lose the point. He [Gumbel] did have a sense of humour, but after an hour that gets a bit wearing.'

Miscellaneous comments

- 'Overall good but perhaps I should have attended with others my own age.'
- 'I think that some people need specific counselling, but use the *Alpha* course instead. I don't know if this is positive.'
- 'The course was good and inspiring whilst attending it. There was no follow-up, which leaves all the emphasis outside the church – disappointing.'
- 'Too optimistic, sees no problems, too glossy in its presentation, and slanted towards young people.'
- 'It would be nice to have a mixture of denominations to make up a more varied group to stir up a little

"controversy". A lot of people come from Catholic back-grounds and all bring the same views. This means that I have not learned anything new as such. It has been more of a refresher. It makes you think again about what you already know.'

Finally, as to the merits of the course, questionnaire respondents were asked if they would like to make any further comments about *Alpha*.

Further comments	%
Would recommend	47
Good evanglical tool	39
Major problems	5
Content of course needs improving	3
Had limitations	3
Too middle class	2

Making a difference

The explicit aims of *Alpha*, as we have seen, are: to allow a forum for people to explore Christianity, to set people on a spiritual journey, and to win converts. The questionnaire addressed these issues. The question was simply posed to respondents: 'Have you become a Christian as a result of taking the *Alpha* course?'

	%
I already am	77
Yes	17
No	4
Not stated	1

It seems that some 17 per cent maintained that they had committed themselves to the faith. The figure, however, is rather misleading. It is evident that the great majority of those answering 'yes' were already in the Church. Their claim to conversion may indicate a greater commitment to the faith. After all, as we have seen, many of those who had enrolled claimed to be on a refresher course or were attempting to find a deeper expression of their belief. Despite this observation, it is clear that a number of 'true' converts were won over. I would estimate this to be 3–4 per cent of the total sampled.

Respondents were also asked the question: 'Has *Alpha* changed your view of Christianity?' The response was as follows:

	%
Yes	44
No	50
Not sure	1
Not stated	4

Apparently, over half those asked were not particularly influenced by *Alpha*. 'Not really. I was already a committed Christian' or 'There was little that I did not know already', were common replies. Among the unchurched a typical response was 'basically no', 'It caused me to challenge my long-term objections to Christianity' or, more brutally, 'It has confirmed my worst fears of Christianity, and Christians'.

The greater majority of those influenced in a positive way by *Alpha* saw it as enhancing their faith:

- 'Not changed my views, only expanded my thoughts.'
- 'Yes. It deepened my faith, extended experiences of fellowship, increased confidence to speak of Jesus.'
- 'Yes, it has helped me root my faith. The Church of England tends to be rather "pick 'n mix" in its attitudes and it's

difficult to decide what one should believe. Having gained good grounding one can move confidently in one's spiritual journey.'

- 'I now concentrate on what unites different denominations. My religion is Christian, not C of E.'
- 'I took confirmation shortly afterwards.'
- 'Not changed my view, but answered questions and a lot of blanks/confusions were sorted out.'
- 'It has explained why Christians behave in a certain manner.'
- 'Yes, I wanted to change from compartmentalising my Christianity to Sunday morning, and instead make it part of my everyday life and thinking. The *Alpha* course has helped me to start this process.'

If not winning too many converts, *Alpha* did seem, according to questionnaire responses, to deepen the spiritual life of over half those who had been through the course, even if the great majority already belonged to a church.

'Has Alpha *influenced your spiritual life?*'	%
Greater spirituality	57
Not at all	16
Greater knowledge	14
Miscellaneous	4
Unsure	1
Not stated	8

Alpha, then, appeared to work, but not in the way intended. Its focus, and hence its perceived advantages, was largely to those already convinced of their faith.

Chapter 7

Alpha on the Ground: the Holy Spirit Weekend

The so-called 'Holy Spirit weekend' is one of the most contro-versial aspects of *Alpha*. Approximately between a third and half-way through the course the guests will usually be invited away on what amounts to a weekend retreat. This is in the company of leaders of the course and anyone else who wants to go along. It is not a compulsory part of the programme, although, more often than not, it will be offered to *Alpha* guests. Again, there are variations on a theme. Quite regu-larly, it is a day, rather than a weekend away that is set aside. Even then, a fairly standard programme will be concentrated into one day's rather frantic round of activities.

Very infrequently the weekend away is not run at all. Gener-ally, this is because the number of guests on the course is too small, or they have other commitments or priorities so that it is not always viable to run it. This is generally inter-preted rather scornfully by course leaders as a lack of commitment to *Alpha*. In contrast, some so-called 'guests', who were really well-established members of a church, would insist on going precisely because they knew what it would entail. A weekend away from life's trials and tribulations, the opportunity for healing, and to be involved in what everybody else was involved in, was the attraction for quite a few.

Some churches, however, will not run the retreat if it is felt that the guests are insufficiently prepared in appreciating what it all amounts to. It is also the case that some guests and even members of a number of churches, so I discovered, may be reluctant to go because they have considerable reservations concerning what might happen. At a United Reformed church in Berkshire, many of the guests on an *Alpha* course (mostly in the church) instigated something of a rebellion when they refused to attend as a result of hearing rumours of what to expect. It was the charismatic element which particularly worried some. An Anglican interviewee expressed her feelings in the light of rumours she had heard about the weekend away: 'I didn't go. I would be embarrassed and uncomfortable with someone laying hands on me. And, the speaking in tongues that happens – I really can't get my head around all that.'

It is the Holy Spirit weekend which critics of *Alpha* have primarily focused upon. One of the principal objections is that it takes people out of their familiar environment and exposes them to manipulation in much the same way as cultist forms of contemporary religion such as Scientology and the Moonies (the Unification Church) do. The fear is that people are removed from their familiar environment and are subjected to indoctrination and what has come to be known in anti-cultist circles as 'love bombing' – where potential converts become the focus of attention and affection. In return, the individual who might be looking into what the religious movement believes, may feel pressured and morally obliged to reciprocate by conforming to what is expected of him/her and ultimately be won over to a set of beliefs they might not otherwise accept.

In the case of *Alpha*, this fear is probably largely unfounded. The *Alpha* course, including the weekend away, is far from cult-like. There is little to compare with the systematic 'brain-washing' techniques that some of the cults employ (and which even in these cases are often exaggerated).[1] However, those of us who have been around in charismatic circles for long enough are aware that undue coercion might be brought to bear on believers and non-believers alike – at least to be involved in activities they would not usually consent to. The dangers of the Holy Spirit weekend were put across in no uncertain terms by one Anglican lady and in such a way as to offer a warning to *Alpha* organisers:

> My biggest argument against *Alpha* was a general feeling that if you hadn't witnessed the Holy Spirit on the appointed weekend then you weren't worthy enough. The weekend was an intense day of being brainwashed. That was the day that it was all leading up to and if you didn't perform then the course leaders thought they had failed. The type of pressure they put on you is like being with the Jehovah's Witnesses. Then they laid hands on me for healing. I was due to have a minor operation on my leg and they thought that I wouldn't have to go. I took it as a bit of an insult.

Signs and some wonders

What, then, does the Holy Spirit weekend entail? Like the rest of the *Alpha* programme, it has evolved over time in both its strategy and content. In terms of the strategy, much is geared to further cement the relationships between guests and course leaders which may have developed in the first few weeks of the *Alpha* course. It does this by attempting to create a conducive ambience – a 'laid-back' environment – to bring a greater cohesion to the *Alpha* group and to allow people to get to know each other a little more. As one enthusiastic lady put it to me:

> A brilliant away day. Felt as though you were in another world. It really gives you a chance to escape from it all. We had a good laugh and lunch at the pub on Saturday. Sunday was just brilliant. You really get to know everyone and the course really does comes alive. I would very much like to go again.

Locations for the Holy Spirit weekend may differ considerably. In my experience they varied from a weekend away at a rural church at the invitation of church members, to a small hotel, or even an animal sanctuary. Wherever it is held, however, the main principal is the same – to have relative seclusion from the outside world. Meals, sleeping arrangements and all other necessities are usually on site, even if there is the odd short excursion to the local pub.

There is considerably more to the weekend away than enhancing the integration of those on the course. The weekend is deliberately planned, at least ideally, to be held at a particular stage of the course and to coincide with teachings on the Holy Spirit and, as one interviewee suggested, 'to bring the course alive'. By the time the guests are invited away they will have had a basic introductory talk on Christianity, teachings on Christ and the atonement, the significance of the Bible and how to read it, how to pray, and how God guides and communicates with the believer. The teachings on the Holy Spirit come next, in the form of three talks on overlapping themes which are the real theological substance over the two days. One variation on this, as was the case with two churches I surveyed, is to customise the course so that the weekend away coincides with later course teachings on healing. The intended effect, however, is the same: to turn some of the theory into practice, or, as it was explained to me by one course leader, 'to provide a practical way of showing Christianity in people's lives'.

The content and structure of the weekend, like much else on the course, is put together in a fairly standardised way. The two days centre on three talks. The first two are given on the Saturday (one in the morning and one in the afternoon), usually with a video presentation followed by discussion, in familiar HTB-form. The first two talks are based on the questions: 'Who is the Holy Spirit?' and 'What does the Holy Spirit do?' For many Christians these themes may seem uncontroversial enough but when unpacked and seen within the context of the time spent away, there is perhaps much which is questionable and unorthodox.

In the first talk, the Holy Spirit is introduced in familiar style with the emphasis on what appears to be a fairly straightforward teaching about the Trinity. The personality of the Holy Spirit is given particular stress, so are teachings alluding to his constant activity and irresistible 'power'. As the *Alpha Manual* puts it, 'He wants to take control'. In the manual, accompanying the text, there is a cartoon of a man with his arm outstretched, trying to resist an invisible force without apparent success.[2] The manual also teaches how, in the Old Testament, 'He [the Holy Spirit] came upon particular people at particular times for particular tasks'.[3] In the New Testament, we are told, ' . . . there is a great activity of the Spirit' and that 'At Pentecost the disciples were filled with the spirit and received – new languages – new boldness – new power'. The conclusion is that 'We live in the age of the Spirit. God has promised to give his Spirit to every Christian'.[4] The emphasis is upon the 'new languages – new boldness – new power' which are available.

After the lunch break, the second talk will then be given. There is not too much which is controversial until, towards the end of the talk, the topic of the charismata is explored – the possibility of speaking in tongues, prophecy, etc., which, it is assumed, are part of the normal Christian experience.[5] At this point, as with most of the first talk on the Holy Spirit, there is a certain amount of suggestibility woven in – particularly the notion that the Holy Spirit is constantly active and hard to resist. This has significance for what follows on the Sunday afternoon. During the Sunday morning the third talk, 'How can I be filled with the Holy Spirit?', begins the day and builds upon Saturday's teachings. Usually, after the third talk, there is time off in the afternoon for leisurely pursuits – perhaps a walk or to talk with others on the course. It is a time meant to be spent in relaxation and reflection. Afternoon tea is followed by a period of prayer and 'Ministry Time', and it is the latter which is perhaps the most controversial aspect of the weekend away.

In order to understand some of the rationale behind the structure and events of the Holy Spirit weekend, particularly its climax in 'Ministry Time', it is necessary to take in a broader understanding of the thinking behind it. In the first place, there is much that happens in Ministry Time which should not surprise anyone who has been familiar with the charismatic movement over the last decade or so. In Chapter 2 we noted the late John Wimber's influence on the movement. At the core of Wimber's teachings was the emphasis on living out the acts and commands of Christ through the experiences of the Holy Spirit, including healing the sick and casting out demons. These were the visible 'signs and wonders' that could convince the disbelieving world and bring church growth. This idea was not entirely original since the teachings had long been developed at the Fuller Seminary where Wimber taught and trained. However, he took some of the doctrines and practices further – to the point that he was effectively disowned by Fuller.

Wimber believed that supernatural phenomena could be manifest if God was given room to act via the faith of believers. This was 'a theology of power' which was furnished with a practical expression through 'power evangelism'. He also developed the notion of 'the divine appointment', which means the appointed time at which God reveals his power to an individual or group through the spiritual gifts or other supernatural phenomena. The Holy Spirit could bring signs and wonders, healings, miracles and other manifestations if people were open to them. The secret, therefore, is to create the right psychological environment for the Holy Spirit to work. This kind of strategy became very popular in many British charismatic churches in the 1980s. While the emphasis upon 'power evangelism' and signs and wonders has declined considerably, the pastoral and emotionally healing element remains. So does the practice of evoking the

Holy Spirit, in which God is asked to minister to those present. It is a practice which engenders a great degree of suggestibility and anticipation.

One of the most vehement critics of Wimber's theology and practice is Martyn Percy.[6] The main objection advanced by Percy is that Wimber (and those inspired by him) had a rather mechanistic approach to the Holy Spirit: that is, if certain procedures are followed, then God is expected to work as if he is some intangible force at the beck and call of believers. Moreover, in preparing the 'divine appointment' – the conditions in which the Holy Spirit works in a human environment – there are various aspects of suggestibility to be observed. This is largely through the lyrics of songs and choruses (and their mantra-type form), group conformity, and the influence of charismatic leaders, which all create an atmosphere that precipitates alleged ecstatic and esoteric manifestations (much of which was typified by the Toronto Blessing). In turn, these 'signs' feed back as a confirmation of the faith of believers and the authority of church leaders. All in all then, a bit of a rather dubious enterprise. Percy's work is a polished and academic critique and an overview does little justice to it. Nonetheless, it does provide constructive insights and, for the sceptic at least, a way of comprehending what Wimber's strategy is all about.

Ministry Time

So-called 'Ministry Time' was one of Wimber's principal contributions to the contemporary charismatic movement and often focused upon various aspects of healing. The attempted healing was usually of an emotional form, although physical healing was sometimes addressed. It is the healing component which has survived in popularity, while Wimber's 'power evangelism' is now somewhat discredited. Ministry Time means administering to the needs of individuals. This frequently involves dealing with spiritual, emotional and psychological problems. A gathered group of believers (perhaps with non-believers), led by a team of 'experienced' Christians, evoke the Holy Spirit. After a period of time, there will be, more often than not, various apparently supernatural phenomena to be observed – perhaps physical shaking, speaking in tongues, weeping, and claims to healing. In the more spectacular manifestations, people may cry, fall to the floor ('resting in the spirit'), or scream with apparent demonic deliverance.

The church members interviewed generally spoke well of Ministry Time. A number of individuals laid claim to receiving spiritual gifts, experiencing healings of an emotional kind and, for one, the claim to a physical healing in the form of a lifelong stammer being overcome. One woman claimed to have conquered her severe jealousy problem and quite a few professed to have been healed of negative memories of the past. However, not all Holy Spirit weekends are so spectacular or noteworthy. Some are quite low-key and may be deliberately aimed at being so on the recognition that emotional outbursts and strange manifestations may be alienating to guests from outside the church and those who have not witnessed it before. The familiar form of Ministry Time, however, is usually replicated on Sunday afternoon on the *Alpha* weekend away. I can describe the events at one retreat.

It is mid-afternoon on a sunny summer's day. There is a slight breeze and a cloudless sky. People wander through the French windows of the drawing room of the large country house that constitutes a Christian retreat. Some latecomers are ushered in politely by the course leaders, who clap their hands in encouragement. Some twelve people sit around in comfortable chairs in a quiet room where there is no disturbance from outside. Conversations die out into whispers. It is a captive audience. There is a quiet anticipation. The curtain is half drawn to keep out the sunlight. The door is closed.

The pastor addresses the small gathering. There are thanks to God for a successful weekend. Joyful moments are briefly recounted. A moment of humour then relaxes the gathering. All is right with the world. A short testimony is given by those who have been on the course before. There is talk of the healing power of the Holy Spirit in people's lives. There are references to past visitations and powerful acts of the conviction of sin and of healing on previous occasions. A number of choruses, accompanied by a guitar, are then softly sung. They refer to God's love and power. After a short period of silence, a prayer for the needs of those present follows. The Holy Spirit is evoked: 'Come, Holy Spirit'.

The course leaders quietly pray. Two church members pray in tongues. In the near silence someone begins to tremble or break into tears. Another gently sobs. Someone comforts them. The team leaders lay hands upon all those present. One waves her outstretched hand around the back of a person's head – praying over him. Another calls on the Holy Spirit to touch those in need. The words 'come Holy Spirit' are heard again. Those present are asked to 'breath in and receive the Spirit'. The crying continues. One person speaks about her personal anguish or some relationship problem, or an emotional hurt from the past. She too is comforted. A church member slides gently from his chair to the floor – 'resting in the spirit'. He lays there for nearly half an hour. Two other church members 'pray over' him. One or two guests, unsure what is going on, ask the course leaders to assure them that things will not get out of hand. They do not. A further forty minutes pass, as tears are wiped away and people slowly get to their feet. Ministry Time peters out and, right on cue, someone brings in the tea and biscuits.[7]

Such experiences witnessed on the weekend away are frequently very personal and subjective. Judgements as to what it all amounts to and what its benefits are remain equally personal and subjective. Certainly, church leaders and course leaders know what to expect and Ministry Time is calculated to have effect. As an Anglican clergyman explained, Ministry Time is

> ... deliberately aimed at getting a feeling of closeness of God. It makes the course mean something – the 'heart stuff' ... it relaxes people, but can frighten others ... it is the core of the course and brings it to life. People are ministered to and God is present. People have a strong sense of being cuddled ... The Holy Spirit comes in a special way, usually a gentle way. But what is being said, however, is 'you've had the theory of Christianity, now here's some of its proof'.

In fact, what is to be expected may be sown into the minds of those present long beforehand. As one course organiser told me: 'We are always a bit worried about how people will see things ... Before the weekend we give the guests a knowledge of what is likely to happen.'

The manifestations can be a difficulty for non-believers and leave some at best perplexed, and at worst feeling disturbed. There are stories of people feeling very uncomfortable at being 'prayed over' and witnessing curious phenomena. One inter-viewee found it all a bit too much:

> The Holy Spirit thing was all a bit weird. We had a session where we could ask the Holy Spirit to come into us by the laying-on-of-hands. I did not feel very comfortable with that at all. The video and all the rest led slowly up to the weekend but the time away really bothered me. I had a bad emotional reaction about my father. It was the same with a woman whose father had MS. She had to leave the room. I remember her crying in the doorway and people having to comfort her. It brings up things that you didn't know you had hurts about. I was upset and the weekend away did nothing

for me. A lot of emotional subjects were being discussed. I think that sometimes people were bordering on a mild hysteria.

Chapter 8

Alpha: Is It Working?

End notes

It is not all evangelising initiatives that have warranted such attention as that received by *Alpha*. And rightly so. Of course, there is a certain amount of hyperbole and not a little razzamatazz. *Alpha News* is full of good reports and self-publicity, with the quotes of politicians, bishops and media personalities from across the globe. There is always news of thousands of people joining *Alpha* courses, and of many conversions. Exaggeration apart, *Alpha*'s scale and influence has been impressive, both nationally and internationally.

There is no doubting that the *Alpha* initiative was intelligently devised. It is relatively cheap and easy to set up and administer. Locally based, it avoids all the disadvantages of the here-today-gone-tomorrow itinerant evangelist ministries, who may be alien to the local context and often bring the emotionalism of orchestrated rallies. There is also certainly an advantage in the supper and the weekend away, which create the right ambience and sustain relationships and networks. There is supportive literature that is generally well written and well presented. It has also been applied with diligence and conviction at the local level by clergy and lay people alike. Indeed, when all is considered, *Alpha* probably constitutes the most successful evangelising campaign for many years. The fact that it has survived in one form or another for two decades, and continues to evolve, is testament to its widespread appeal. It will, at least the evidence suggests, continue in one form or another for some time in the future.

Alpha, to some extent at least, is consumer led. To that end the course continues to be refined, taking into account people's experiences, whether of those who run it or their 'guests'. It is also, as we have noted, suitable for most churches and denominations; it is ecumenical in its nature and user-friendly. The programme has thus brought churches in Britain together in a common endeavour. Although some, for largely theological reasons, choose to remain outside of its influence, *Alpha* has brought an increasing sense of unity and purpose. This new-found collective spirit between the churches may be interpreted as one of the advantages of *Alpha*. However, as the sociologist Bryan Wilson once suggested, ecumenical initiatives are really a sign of the weakness of the churches.[1] Ever beleaguered, the denominations of today no longer bicker about differences of doctrine or practice; they are less likely to draw up barriers between each other or experience sectarian divisions. They no longer have the strength to proclaim their distinctiveness. Hedged in by the secular world, there is comfort and protection in collaboration. In this sense *Alpha*, since it is an ecumenical initiative, may provide a useful barometer of the condition of Christianity in Britain and elsewhere.

There are other ways in which *Alpha* can be said to signify the state of the contemporary churches. Perhaps, above all, it can be seen as utilising all the insights and experiences which have been gathered over several decades. Hence, it is probably the best evangelising tool presently on offer because it makes full use of sociological and psychological approaches and displays an understanding of contemporary culture and social change. *Alpha*, then, recognises the scepticism of the modern (or is it post-modern?) world, the importance of belonging, and the all-pervading consumerist culture of Western society. It thus tries to be 'relevant to modern man' in that it attempts a safe atmosphere for proselytisation and endeavours to explore key Christian doctrines in an allegedly sensitive and constructive way. Commenting on the logic behind *Alpha*, Damian Thompson, a freelance writer specialising in religious matters, has remarked that its ingenuity lies in its simplicity and ability to reach people 'where they are'. He states:

> British Christianity has stumbled across the big idea that has eluded it for most of its feeble Decade of Evangelism. It is not so much a big idea, so much as a small one brilliantly executed. Its popularity owes little to mission strategies or the thaumaturgical [wonder-working] extravagances of the Toronto Blessing. Its milieu is mundane and domestic.[2]

The great strength of *Alpha*, however, may also be said to be its major weakness – that is, its simplicity and attempt to be congruent with all things contemporary. Being 'relevant to modern man' and putting the gospel message across in a simple way may mean leaving little scope for exploring personal experiences, Church history and the wide-ranging nature of the faith. In essence, it is sold and marketed effectively but sometimes it gives the impression of offering a cheap package deal or, to quote Martyn Percy, it endeavours to provide 'a bargain-break weekend for two in eternity'.[3] Being simple also means that the *Alpha* programme sets and answers its own questions. It over-simplifies sophisticated critiques of Christianity and then destroys them. It allows little discussion of the complex issues. It is, then, in its own way, hermetically foolproof. Of course, there are post-*Alpha* programmes which may discuss some issues at greater length. However, they tend to display the same weaknesses.

Winning converts?

Given all its claimed advantages and widespread use, the question may be asked whether *Alpha* is reversing church decline, reinvigorating the faith, and changing the fortunes of Christianity in an age of disbelief and scepticism. Certainly some are optimistically convinced that it has the potential to do so. We may note the observance of another independent source. Clifford Longley, a well-known and respected religious affairs writer, on one occasion dedicated his weekly column in the *Daily Telegraph* to the subject of the *Alpha* course. The article is frequently reprinted in *Alpha* publications to encourage those involved in the initiative. Longley's tone is optimistic in his declaration that *Alpha* is

> an unqualified triumph.The reconversion of
> England . . . is suddenly almost believable . . . It
> makes the church seem professional, competent, self-
> confident and up to date . . . It is an idea whose time
> is long overdue.

Such near-euphoria is, to my mind, unfounded and misleading. It is true that *Alpha* has made considerable impact but this is only relatively speaking when measured against other evangelising initiatives in recent years. That is not saying a great deal. *Alpha*, given the number of people enrolled on the courses nationwide is still 'small time'. True, there are many stories of conversion through *Alpha* courses, although I have not seen any statistics indicating how many. The reality is that *Alpha* is probably not winning a substantial number of new converts, at least in Britain.

There are various reasons why this is so. The first observation is that 'cold' advertising does not work – that is, the use of posters and leaflets to 'sell' the faith. In that sense the national initiative launched in 1998 has not been successful. Saturation advertising may work in selling commercial products but this is observably not the case with religion. It may simply be that the 'supply-side', the *Alpha* organisers, have not been sufficiently slick or imaginative. This remains a subject for debate. The evidence, it seems, is not good. Of the four churches I surveyed in my sample, all of whom had advertised in this way over a number of years, only one person was ever converted after being prompted to join *Alpha* by the attraction of a message on a poster. In Wokingham, a prosperous town just outside of Reading, some 22,000 leaflets were distributed by a number of churches working together. Only five people joined up as a result. As elsewhere, the experience of these churches was that the great bulk of people who signed up for *Alpha* were encouraged to do so through established relationships and social networks.

There are plenty of people who have never heard of *Alpha*. There are many too who fail to respond. It may well be that there is not the 'consumer demand' for what it has to offer. No amount of advertising or business strategy is going to change that fact. *Alpha* may be winning a small number of converts. However, it is certainly not replenishing the ranks of those who have left the churches in recent years. Indeed, we must look at the bigger picture. Statistics produced in January 2000 by MARC Europe, some fifteen months after *Alpha* was launched, showed further national church attendance decline. The proportion of people in England and Wales who attend church on Sunday is probably now less than 7 per cent. The same report suggested that if present trends continue then it is feasible that by the year 2020, the attendance at churches on a Sunday may be down to merely 1 per cent. This raises the question as to whether the churches should be as concerned with retaining members as much as winning over new ones.

It is probably unfair, however, to take a simple snapshot of *Alpha* in terms of reversing church attendance. Converts are not expected to be won overnight. In terms of winning converts, Holy Trinity, Brompton, has been more successful largely because it has had more time to develop its courses and establish networks with those outside the church. It also has to be remembered that *Alpha* is geared to winning souls but not necessarily in the short term. It attempts to inform the uninformed about Christianity. It is a basic course to explore the faith – to encourage people to think about the merits of Christianity, and in doing so it may spark a spiritual journey. The harvest may come later. I think, however, that this is unlikely. This is not entirely the Church's fault. As one clergyman put it to me with classic charismatic jargon:

> It is not for the want of trying. In Britain we have good church leaders, advanced marketing skills, and all other resources for a revival. The problem is that there is a spirit of cynicism over the nation. A rational spirit of disbelief.

The stark reality is that the basis of belief and belonging may not be there. I personally doubt whether much of an untapped or potential spirituality exists. Neither is it likely that any of the other expressions of new religiosity in the form of New Religious Movements or the New Age are going to fill the gap. We live in a profoundly secular society. This side of all-out war or a global epidemic, a religious, specifically Christian, revival is unlikely. *Alpha* may have attracted the earnest, unconverted seeker through its dragnet, and brought some prodigals back home. But if it is the best the contemporary Church has to offer, in terms of marketing techniques and applied sociology and social psychology, then even that may not be enough.

Another observation is that *Alpha* is more appealing to some rather than others. This may be because it is rooted in the charismatic movement. Certainly, *Alpha* does not really attract the poorest section of the population. The obvious deduction is that its culture is middle class and appeals primarily to middle-class people. This had always been one of the major limitations of the charismatic movement. Back in 1978 the leading Baptist charismatic Douglas McBain had spoken about 'the hard places' to which evangelism needed to direct itself in earnest: the inner-city areas and the under-privileged sections of British society.[4] Those who had little stake in this world also had little hope for the next. No recent large-scale evangelising programme devised has reached this constituency. Neither does *Alpha*. Its intellectual level, its cultural trappings and general orientation is more likely to appeal to 'middle-England' – the relatively well educated and moderately affluent. The fact is that in as much as *Alpha* is making converts, it appears merely to add to the middle-class cohorts of the charismatic movement.

There is another matter to consider. It may be one thing getting people to an *Alpha* course. It is another keeping them there. The drop-out rate, estimated by Holy Trinity, Brompton, at about 30 per cent, is obviously high. My research took some account of those who left. I can relate the situation in one church I surveyed. In 1999, it ran two courses. The statistics below show what happened to the 39 people who enrolled. This example is not untypical.

24	already in the church
10	dropped out
1	had conversion experience and joined the church after *Alpha* course
4	were never seen again

The fact that just one person was converted may be a reason for rejoicing. However, the question is why people drop out, or, for that matter, endure the course but are not converted? Is the message irrelevant? Is the *Alpha* package unattractive? Is the church environment alienating? The evidence of this study is that a good many are lost in the first few weeks. It was hard to trace, and even harder to get to talk to people who had dropped out. However, I did manage to speak to a handful of individuals who forwarded the following reasons for deciding to leave.

- Sheer endurance of the course: 'too much like hard work'.
- 'It was church just as I remembered it, it did nothing special for me.'
- Found the Holy Spirit day disturbing.
- Did not like the Bible readings.
- Did not like the video.
- Found the environment intimidating.

People are, however, attracted to *Alpha* and for specific reasons. It is obviously dealing with the needs of some. For a few, the socially isolated, it provides company. Of course, in itself this is not a bad thing. In some cases it may be appealing to those with emotional and psychological problems. Again, who could complain about its beneficial effects in this respect? This was not, however, what *Alpha* really intended. Neither was its prime function to deal with the needs of those already in the church. Rather, the aim is to win converts. At least according to my sample, very few new converts were actually won (some 3–4 per cent of those enrolled on the course). Seeing that *Alpha* was not attracting those outside the church, a House Church leader I spoke to told me that his *Alpha* course now insists that those in the church should not join. The problem was, he explained, that courses were often undersubscribed and frequently cancelled.

The pastor at Free Church #2 explained to me that *Alpha* was primarily 'a way of confirming the faith of those already converted, teaching more about the basics, and bringing a greater encounter with God'. This should not necessarily surprise us. In earlier times Billy Graham-type campaigns had a different purpose from those envisaged by the organisers. As one famous sociological study has shown, they were always more likely to attract the already converted and functioned more as 'status confirmation rituals' for the faithful.

In short, they provided a sense of belonging, identity and revival for those already converted, or brought backsliders back into the fold.[5] *Alpha* largely does this through a charismatic form of Christianity.

Arguably *Alpha*, like the Toronto Blessing which preceded it, could turn out to be something of a fad albeit a more constructive one. This I doubt. However, *Alpha's* net effect is in extending charismatic Christianity to the churches, including those previously untouched by the Renewal movement. According to interviews and questionnaires, it was apparently the charismatic element which provided a deeper expression of the faith. Charismatic Christianity therefore continues, for good or for bad, to carry on the same function that it has for nearly four decades in spiritually reinvigorating those already in the churches. This has been by far its major achievement.

Alpha may be something of a victory for the charismatics. However, some might argue that this is damaging because its theological content is askew and, for that reason, it may be doomed to failure. This is not something that I can comment on. However, I do note the absence of alternatives. There are one or two dotted about, such as the more user-friendly and less objectionable *Erasmus* programme. These are even more small-time. Within evangelical Protestantism there are theological opponents to *Alpha*. There is talk of non-charismatic evangelicals putting their own programme together: something which, it is frequently claimed, will be more orthodox and closer to a 'truer' Christianity. We wait in earnest anticipation. In the meantime, the charismatics have the upper hand.

Some personal observations

As an outsider, I am fairly well predisposed towards *Alpha*. I did not experience intimidation or brain-washing. I never felt anything but welcomed by honest and earnest people who ran the course. However, I am left with the thought as to whether *Alpha* really is the best evangelising initiative that the Church has to offer. As far as the content was concerned, it was instantly recognisable as fairly traditional Christianity, albeit with overtly charismatic elements. To be more user-friendly perhaps, the more objectionable topics on the charismata and healing should be taken out (or at least considered in a follow-up course), which would also have the advantage of shortening a course that is probably too long. Then there is the Holy Spirit weekend which has met with such a mixed reception. Like many things I have seen in charismatic circles over the last few years, the weekend away has its good and bad points. As with the Toronto Blessing, it could be beneficial to some if it is handled constructively. Very often the Holy Spirit weekend is not. Above all, it is likely to alienate outsiders if course leaders are not discerning. A weekend away from the hustle and bustle of everyday life is surely to be valued. It is how the time is used which needs to be thoroughly appraised.

Ultimately, *Alpha* should be judged by what it claims to do. It presents itself as an opportunity to *explore* Christianity. In my experience of the course, however, exploration was often replaced by one degree or another of indoctrination. In short, the difficulty I had was that *it* set the agenda to a far greater extent than necessary. Each week the course presented its own theme from a Christian point of view, which was held, by definition, to be invariably true. The onus was on the guests, should they wish to participate in discussion, to disprove the evidence or enter into contention by forceful argument. In the first few weeks this type of approach can be intimidating and probably explains the high drop-out rate at this stage.

Alpha also assumes too much knowledge. Since, at least in the churches I surveyed, most of those on the course were already committed Christians, they would not have difficulty in following the arguments or finding the relevant biblical passages (although some notably did). A course for beginners, however, has to be a bit more basic and use a few more imaginative ways of exploring what Christianity is about. Forty minutes of Nicky Gumbel dictating what is self-evidently true is not always helpful. Moreover, video presentations are not the only medium which could be used with a little more imagination. However, to encourage this would lead to considerable variation at the local level and disturb the standard product of *Alpha*, which is partly one of the reasons for its appeal. On the other hand, however, to encourage innovation may mean that HTB might lose its control over the course and hence its high profile.

If it were to be a genuine course for beginners then in some respects *Alpha* needs to be in many ways different, more radical and more challenging. At the moment it is something of a catch-all for believers and non-believers alike. This explains its relative popularity. If it continues to operate, as it does, largely for the converted, then it should be called something else. If it is a revision of Christianity that is required then it should be called 'a revision course'. If people are seeking to develop their faith, then the course should be called something equally appropriate. If people need pastoral care, then the local church should put on healing sessions. If they want company, then there should be a 'meet people in your church you have not spoken to for twenty years' course. The designation 'Alpha' suggests a beginning, and that should be where it starts, with something more rudimentary, more basic. As it stands, *Alpha* entails a hit-and-miss strategy. To put it succinctly, organisers must recognise quite how secular today's society has become.

It is, of course, very easy to criticise if you do not have anything to suggest on your own behalf by way of an alternative. There are plenty of critics out there who often have nothing themselves to offer. *Alpha*, in true McDonaldization fashion, largely has a monopoly. There is no reason why it should. Perhaps it is worth considering the 'Alternative Alpha

Course' for those who have never even heard of Christianity. How about the following, in a rather shortened version of an introduction to the faith?

The Alternative Alpha Course

Week 1 *Christianity: boring, untrue and irrelevant?*
What *is* the relevance of Christianity today?

Week 2 *Who is God? Who is Jesus? What is the Bible all about?*
The Word needs to be explained, mysteries explored. It is *assumed* that people have rudimentary knowledge. This ain't necessarily so.

Week 3 *Christianity and other religions*
What do other faiths believe? What is special about Christianity?

Week 4 *The Christian life*
How should people lead their lives? How do they deal with ethical issues and moral dilemmas?

Week 5 *Suffering and the lot of man*
How did suffering get here and what can Christians do to ease suffering in the world?

Week 6 *What do we make of Church history?*
Why has the history of the Church been a bit of a mess? What are the lessons to learn?

Week 7 *Why do Christians disagree?*
Why do they bicker so much? Why do some think that they have got the truth while others have an incomplete bit of it?

Week 8 *Christianity in the world today*
Where does it all go from here? Where would you like to go?

Well, just a few thoughts. In the meantime, anyone for *Alpha?*

Notes

Foreword
1. In the United States tele-evangelism can trace its lineage to urban mission.
2. Though the thrust of Grace Davie's book is that belief is wider and more enduring than church membership: *Religion in Britain since 1945: Believing without Belonging*, Oxford: Blackwell, 1994.
3. *The Logic of Evangelism*, Hodder & Stoughton, 1989, Chs 6 and 7.

Introduction
1. These findings were first presented at the British Sociological Association Religion Study Group conference, The University of Durham, April 1999.

Chapter 1: 'Alpha: I've Heard of That!'
1. The statistics are from *Alpha News* (November 1998 – February 1999), no.17, p.1. *Alpha News* is published three times a year by Holy Trinity, Brompton.
2. Quoted in an article by Dominic Kennedy in *The Times* (9th September 1998).
3. These figures may be an underestimation since some churches do not register their courses with the national organisers, Holy Trinity, Brompton. There are a number of reasons for this. The principal one appears to be because a fair few churches have customised the course, against Holy Trinity's wishes and, for that reason, prefer not to be formally associated.
4. From *Alpha: God Changing Lives*, published by Holy Trinity, Brompton.
5. *Alpha News* (March–June 1999), no.18, p.1.
6. *Alpha News* (November 1998–February 1999), no.17. In Lewis prison on the Isle of Wight there has apparently been a very large revival, although it is hard to say how much is *Alpha* propaganda.
7. Interview with Ben Pollard at Holy Trinity, Brompton, 13th November 1998.
8. P. Brierley (1991) *Prospects for the Nineties: Trends and Tables From the English Church Census with Denominations and Churchmanships*, Eltham: MARC Europe.

9. P. Brierley (1992) *Christian England. What the 1989 English Church Census Reveals*, London: MARC Europe.
10. Brierley (1992) pp.30–32.
11. Brierley (1992) pp.30–31.
12. Brierley (1992) p.33.
13. See, for example, Robert Bellah (1965) 'Religious Evolution', *American Sociological Review*, 29 (3), pp.358-74, and more recently R. Stark and W. Bainbridge (1985) *The Future of Religion*, Berkeley, Cal: University of California Press.
14. G. Davie (1994) *Religion in Britain since 1945: Believing Without Belonging*, Oxford: Blackwell.
15. Quoted in an article by Dominic Kennedy in *The Times*, 9th September 1998.
16. Sandy Millar, *Alpha: God Changing Lives*, Holy Trinity, Brompton.

Chapter Two: The Background to *Alpha*

1. For an overview of Wimber's ministry see M. Percy (1996) *Words, Wonder and Power: Understanding Christian Fundamentalism and Revivalism*, London: SPCK; D. McBain (1997) 'Mainline Charismatics: Some Observations of Baptist Renewal' in S. Hunt, M. Hamilton and T.Walter (eds), *Charismatic Christianity: Sociological Perspectives*, Basingstoke: Macmillan, pp.43–59.
2. For example, D. Snow and R. Machelek (1984) 'The Sociology of Conversion', *Annual Review of Sociology*, 10, pp.167–90; A. Greil and D. Rudy (1984) 'What Have We Learned From Process Models of Conversion? An Examination of Ten Case Studies', *Sociological Focus*, 17 (4), pp.305–21.
3. For general reading on the global charismatic movement, see H. Cox (1994) *Fire From Heaven. The Rise of Pentecostal Spirituality and the Reshaping of Religion in the Twenty-First Century*, Reading, Mass: Addison Publishing Company, and D. Martin (1990) *Tongues of Fire. The Explosion of Pentecostalism in Latin America*, Oxford: Blackwell.
4. P. Wagner (1988) *The Third Wave of the Holy Spirit*, Ann Arbor: Servant Press.
5. P. Brierley (1992) *Christian England. What the 1989 English Church Census Reveals*, London: MARC Europe, p.116.
6. M. Weber (1965) *The Sociology of Religion*, Methuen: London.
7. For a detailed account of Restorationism and its development into the New Churches, see A. Walker (1999) *Restoring the Kingdom*, London: Eagle.
8. Cox (1994) p.272.
9. For more academic accounts of the Toronto Blessing, see S. Hunt (1995) 'The Toronto Blessing'. A Rumour of Angels', *The Journal of Contemporary Religion*, 10 (3), pp.257–72; M. Percy (1966) *The Toronto Blessing*, Oxford: Latimer Press; P. Richter (1995) 'God Is Not a Gentleman!' in S. Porter and P. Richter (eds) (1995) *The Toronto Blessing. Or is It?*, London: Darton, Longman & Todd.
10. *Daily Mail*, 10th May 1994.

11. *Jesus Life* (1995), July, p.12.
12. Hunt (1995).
13. Hunt (1995).
14. Richter (1995)
15. Walker (1999).
16. Post-Toronto Blessing, some esoteric phenomena have continued. One craze in some charismatic churches in the late 1990s was that of 'teeth-filling' – a belief that God was filling the teeth of believers with gold. See A. Walker (1999) *From Base Metal to Gold: Theological Reflections on the Gold Teeth Filling Phenomenon*, www.Ship-of-Fools.com.

Chapter Three: *Alpha* – Strategy, Content and a Few Controversies

1. I have had little personal contact with HTB over the last few years. Previously, I found the church leaders polite, but not always as forthcoming to outside enquiry as they might be.
2. G. Ritzer (1996) *The McDonaldization of Society*, New York: Pine Forge Press, p.1.
3. P. Cook (1998) '*Alpha* Courses: Some Observations and Misgivings', *Challenge Weekly*, 27th November.
4. M. Percy (1998) 'Join-the-Dots Christianity. Assessing Alpha', *Reviews in Religion and Theology*, May.
5. C. Hand, 'Is *Alpha* leading people astray?', *Alpha* website, 1999.
6. J. Hunter (1987) *Evangelicalism: The Coming Generations*, Chicago: Chicago University Press.
7. Percy (1999) p.14.
8. Quoted in an article by Dominic Kennedy in *The Times*, 9th September 1998.

Chapter Four: Who Adopts *Alpha* and Why?

1. Maidenhead was the subject of a report in *The Economist* (27th June 1998, pp.37–8). The theme of the article was that of church decline, the fortunes of different churches, and ethnic religious pluralism. It includes a mention of the introduction of *Alpha* by a number of churches. Maidenhead has a population of around 50,000.
2. *Alpha Magazine*, 1965, May, 6 and 9. (This magazine should not be confused with the *Alpha* course or any of its publications.)
3. This, and a number of other unashamedly charismatic Anglican churches, uses a publication called *Briefings* after the *Alpha* course finishes in order to supplement its charismatic element. The same publication also seems to have been adopted by some Roman Catholic groups.

Chapter Five: Who Joins *Alpha* and Why?

1. These, and other statistics quoted in this book, have been 'rounded off'.

2. P. Richter and L. Francis (1998) *Gone But Not Forgotten. Church Leaving and Returning*, London: Darton, Longman & Todd, pp.59–63.
3. Richter and Francis (1998) p.61.
4. Brierley (1992) *Christian England.*
5. M. Neitz (1987) *Charisma and Community: A Study of Religious Commitment Within Charismatic Renewal*, Oxford: Transaction Books.
6. R. Wallis (1984) *The Elementary Formers of New Religious Life*, London: Routledge & Kegan Paul.
7. T. Walter (1990) 'Why Are Most Church-Goers Women?', *Vox Evangelica*, 5, pp.599–625.
8. HTB is somewhat different here. The average age of an *Alpha* guest is 27 (according to the article 'Now God is Cool' by Sue Arnold in the *Observer* newspaper, 11th June 2000). This is part of a profile of a distinct clientele.
9. R. Bibby (1977) 'Going, Going, Gone: The Impact of Geographical Mobility on Religious Involvement', *Review of Religious Research*, 38, pp.289–307 (quoted in Brierley, 1992, pp.91–2).
10. Richter and Francis (1998), especially Chapter 6.

Chapter Six: *Alpha* on the Ground: Some Observations

1. M. Abrow (1995) 'Globalisation' in R.Brym (ed.) *New Society: Sociology for the 21st Century*, Toronto: Harcourt Brace, pp.1–25; R. Robertson (1992) *Globalisation: Social Theory and Global Culture*, London: Sage, pp.19, 172.
2. Sandy Millar, copyright statement of *Alpha*, Holy Trinity, Brompton.

Chapter Seven: *Alpha* on the Ground: the Holy Spirit Weekend

1. Peter Cook, in his article '*Alpha* Courses: Some Observations and Misgivings' (*Challenge Weekly*, 27th November 1999), presents a useful criticism of the weekend away, especially the emphasis of waiting on the spirit and speaking in tongues.
2. *Alpha Manual*, p.30.
3. *Alpha Manual*, p.31.
4. *Alpha Manual*, p.32.
5. *Alpha Manual*, p.35.
6. M. Percy (1996) *Words, Wonders and Power. Understanding Contemporary Christian Fundamentalism and Revivalism*, London: SPCK.
7. Among Roman Catholics there may be prayers of confession (in Roman Catholic circles the weekends are often run by a priest) during Ministry Time.

Chapter Eight: *Alpha:* Is It Working?

1. B. Wilson (1966) *Religion in a Secular Society*, London: C. A. Watts.
2. Damian Thompson in *The Times*, 2nd February 1998.
3. M. Percy (1998) 'Join-the-Dots Christianity. Assessing Alpha', reviews in *Religion and Theology*, May, p.16.

4. D. McBain (1978) 'The Spirit's Call to the Hard Places', *Renewal*, 74, pp.28–31.
5. K. Lang and G. Lang (1960) 'Decisions for Christ: Billy Graham in NYC', in A. Vidich and D. White (eds) *Identity and Anxiety*, New York: Free Press.